THE CATHOLIC UNIVERSITY OF AMERICA
CANON LAW STUDIES
Number 109

THE ADMINISTRATION OF TEMPORAL GOODS IN RELIGIOUS INSTITUTES

A DISSERTATION

Submitted to the Faculty of Canon Law of the Catholic University of America in Partial Fulfillment of the Requirements for the Degree of

DOCTORATE OF CANON LAW

BY

JAMES EDWARD MCMANUS, C.SS.R., J.C.L.
Of the Baltimore Province

THE CATHOLIC UNIVERSITY OF AMERICA
WASHINGTON, D. C.
1937

Imprimi Potest:

Brooklynii, die 20 Aprilis 1937.

ANDREAS B. KUHN, C.Ss.R.,

Provincialis.

Nihil Obstat:

Washingtonii, die 7 Maii 1937.

VALENTINUS T. SCHAFF, O.F.M., J.C.D.,

Censor Deputatus.

Imprimi Potest:

Baltimorae, die 4 Maii 1937.

✠ MICHAEL J. CURLEY,

Archiepiscopus Baltimorensis.

PRINTED BY

THE UNIVERSITY PRESS

BROOKLAND, D. C.

AD
C. Ss. R.

FOREWORD

Temporal goods are the stay and support of temporal existence. Their use is evidently necessary not only for individual needs but also for the needs of groups and associations united for a common purpose. If, when united for a common purpose, a group of individuals has received the approval of the ecclesiastical authority, their common property acquires a quality or characteristic that is worthy of special consideration. It becomes ecclesiastical property, that is, the property of an ecclesiastical moral person, and as such becomes subject to the laws of the Church regulating the use and administration of church property.

This monograph treats only of church property, and therefore is not concerned with the private property of individual religious. However, it does not attempt to explain the general subject of ecclesiastical property. The field is too large and the matter too complicated to be treated in a single dissertation. Even the particular subject of religious ecclesiastical property is too extensive to admit of adequate treatment within the limits of a single volume. Such a subject could be treated under the aspect of the civil law, or from the viewpoint of particular religious law, or finally, in the light of the Code. The Civil Law phase of this subject has been entirely omitted in this dissertation. The matter is too complex and would require a special study even to treat of the Civil Law in the United States. Similarly the particular law of religious institutes has been left out of consideration in writing this dissertation for the reason that it would lack importance for the general reader. This dissertation confines itself to a study of the general laws of the Church in as far as they concern the administration of property in religious institutes. Its purpose is to explain these laws; to show their application; and to set forth and analyze the opinions of the different authors in regard to those parts of the law which admit of different interpretations.

The subject has been treated before. The works of Fathers Vromant and Larraona in this field are outstanding, and the writer is indebted to these authors for much of the material found in these pages. However the subject is not yet free of difficulties and the present dissertation is an attempt to throw additional light on some of them. In treating these difficulties an effort has been made to adopt a positive stand. It is hoped that this will not be interpreted as an intolerant attitude towards the views of others. The reader should therefore keep in mind the controversial character of much of the material treated in this work. It is also proper to call the reader's attention to the fact that besides what is stated in these pages it may also be necessary at times to apply to particular cases the prescripts of civil law or of particular religious law.

The writer takes this occasion to express sincere thanks to Very Rev. Andrew B. Kuhn, C.Ss.R., his provincial superior, for the oportunity given him for advanced study in Canon Law. He also acknowledges with appreciation and sincere thanks the assistance given him by the Faculty of the School of Canon Law of the Catholic University of America.

TABLE OF CONTENTS

CHAPTER II

CHAPTER III

CHAPTER IV

CHAPTER V

CHAPTER VI

CHAPTER VII

BIBLIOGRAPHY

Sources

Acta Apostolicae Sedis (*AAS*), Romae, 1909—.

Acta et Decreta Concilii Plenarii Baltimorensis Tertii, Baltimore, Murphy, 1886.

Acta et Decreta Sacrorum Conciliorum Recentiorum (*Collectio Lacensis*), 7 vols., Friburgi Brisgoviae, 1870-1890.

Acta Sanctae Sedis(*ASS*), 41 vols., Romae, 1865-1908.

Bouscaren, T., *The Canon Law Digest*, Milwaukee, Bruce, 1934.

Bullarium Franciscanum, 7 vols., Romae, 1759-1908.

Bullarium Romanum, 24 vols., Editio Taurinensis, 1857-1872.

Bullarii Romani Continuatio, 13 vols., Prati, 1845-1854.

Codicis Iuris Canonici Fontes, 7 vols., Romae, 1923-1935.

Codex Theodosianus, (Krueger-Mommsen-Meyer), 3 vols., Berolini, 1905.

Collectanea Sacrae Congregationis de Propaganda Fide, 2 vols., Romae, 1907.

Concilii Tridentini Actorum, Pars Sexta, Complectens Acta Post Sessionem Sextam (*XXII*), *usque ad finem Concilii*, collegit, edidit, illustravit, Stephanus Ehses, Friburgi Brisgoviae, 1924.

Corpus Iuris Canonici, editio Lipsiensis secunda post Aemilii Ricteri curas . . . instruxit Aemilius Friedberg, 2 vols., Leipsic, 1879-1881.

Corpus Iuris Civilis (Krueger-Mommsen-Schoell-Kroll), 5. ed., 3 vols., Berlin, Weidman, 1928.

Denziger, H.-Bannwart, C., *Enchiridion Symbolorum*, 16. et 17 ed., Friburgi Brisgoviae, Herder, 1928.

Harduinus, J., *Acta Conciliorum et Epistolae Decretales ac Constitutiones Summorum Pontificum*, 12 vols., Parisiis, 1715.

Kirch, C., *Enchiridion Fontium Historiae Ecclesiasticae Antiquae*, 4. ed., Friburgi Brisgoviae, Herder, 1923.

Mansi, Joannes Dominicus, *Sacrorum Conciliorum Nova et Amplissima Collectio*, 59 vols., Parisiis, 1901-1927.

Migne, Jacques Paul, *Patrologia Graeca*(*MPG*), 161 vols., Paris, 1858-1864.

Migne, Jacques Paul, *Patrologia Latina*(*MPL*), 221 vols., Paris, 1847-1870.

Normae secundum quas S. Cong. Episcoporum et Regularium procedere solet in Approbandis Novis Institutis votorum simpicium, Romae, 1901.

Pallotini, S., *Collectio omnium conclusionum et resolutionum quae in causis propositis apud Sacrum Congregationem Cardinalium S. Concilii Tridentini interpretum prodierunt ab eius institutione anno 1564 ad annum 1860*, 17 vols., 1868-1893.

Woywod, S., *Canonical Decisions of the Holy See*, New York, Wagner, 1933.

AUTHORS

Acta Congressus Juridici Internationalis, 2 vols., Romae, 1935-1936.

[Bachofen,] Charles Augustine, *A Commentary on the New Code of Canon Law,* 8 vols., St. Louis, Herder, 1926.

Balthasar, Karl, *Geschichte Des Armutsstreites im Franziskanerorden bis zum Konzil von Vienne,* Muenster, 1911.

Barbosa, Augostino, *Iuris Ecclesiastici Universi, Libri Tres,* Lugduni, 1634.

Baynes, N. H., *Constantine the Great and the Christian Church,* British Academy, London, 1929.

Benedict XIV, *De Synodo Dioecesana,* 4 vols., Lovanii, 1763.

Benedict XIV, *Institutiones Ecclesiasticae,* Prati, 1844.

Berutti, C., *Institutiones Iuris Canonici,* vol. III (*De Religiosis*), Taurini, Marietti, 1936.

Bianchi, A., *Potesta della Chiesa,* tom. 4, Roma, 1756.

Boudinhon, A., *Biens d'eglises et peines canoniques,* Paris,, 1909.

Bouix, D., *Tractatus de Jure Regularium,* 2. ed. 2 vols., Bruxellis, 1867.

Brown, B. F., *The Canonical Juristic Personality with Special Reference to Its Status in the United States of America,* Washington, 1927.

Butler, E. C., *Benedictine Monachism,* London, 1919.

Cambridge Medieval History, The, 8 vols., New York, Macmillan, 1936.

Cappello, F. M., *De Censuris iuxta Codicem Juris Canonici,* Taurini, 1919.

Catholic Encyclopedia, The, 16 vols., New York, 1907-1914.

Chelodi, J., *Jus de Personis,* 2 ed., Tridenti, 1927.

Cicognani, A., *Canon Law,* Philadelphia, Dolphin Press, 1934.

Cleary, J., *Canonical Limitations on the Alienation of Church Property,* Washington, D. C., 1936.

Cocchi, Guidus, *Commentarium in Codicem Iuris Canonici,* 9 vols., Taurini, Marietti, 1924-1927.

Conte a Coronata, M., *Institutiones Iuris Canonici,* Taurini, Marietti, 1931.

Creusen, J., *Religieux et Religieuses d'apres le Droit Ecclesiastique,* 13. ed., Bruxelles; 1924.

De Lugo, J., *Disputationes Scholasticae et Morales,* 9. ed., Parisiis, 1869.

De Meester, A., *Iuris Canonici Compendium, Brugis,* 1921-1927.

Dernburg, Heinrich von, *System des Roemischen Rechts,* 2 vols., Berlin 1912.

Doheny, W. J., *Church Property: Modes of Acquisition,* Washington, D. C., 1927.

Duchesne, L., *Origines du Culte Chretien,* Paris, 1908.

Dudden, F. H., *St .Gregory the Great, His Place in History and Thought,* London, 1905.

Felder, H., *Ideals of St. Francis of Assisi,* New York, 1925.

Ferraris, F., *Bibliotheca Canonica Iuridica Moralis Theologica necnon Ascetica Polemica Rubristica Historica,* 9 vols., Romae, 1891.

Gasquet, Abbot, *English Monastic Life,* New York, 1905.

Giraldus, Ubaldus, *Expositio Iuris Pontificii,* 2 vols., Romae, 1829.

Grupp, *Kulturgeschichte der roemischen Kaiserzeit,* 3 vols., Muenchen, 1903.

Hefele, J. C., *Conciliengeschichte,* 2. ed., 9 vols., Freiburg, im Br., Herder, 1873-1890.

Heimbucher, Max., *Die Orden und Kongregationen der Katholischen Kirche,* 3. ed., 2 vols., Paderborn, 1933.

Hollweck, J., *Die Kirchlichen Strafgesetze,* Mainz, 1899.

Holzapfel, Heribert, *Manuale Historiae Ordinis Fratrum Minorum,* Freiburg im Br., Herder, 1909.

Jansen, J., *Ordensrecht,* 2. ed., Paderborn, Schoeningh, 1920.

Koch, Hugo, *Virgines Christi,*. Leipzig, 1907.

Ladeuze, Paulinus, *De Instituto Coenobitico Sancti Pachomii,* Louvain, 1898.

Leage, R. W., *Roman Private Law,* 2. ed., London, Macmillan, 1930.

Leipoldt, Joannes, *Schneute von Atripe und die Entstehung des National Aegyptischen Christentums,* Leipzig, 1903.

Linsenmann, J., *Denkschrift über die Frage der Männerorden in Württemberg,* Stuttgart, 1892.

Logeman, H., *The Rule of St. Benet,* London, N. Truebner & Co., 1888.

Maroto, P., *Institutiones Iuris Canonici,* 3. ed., 2 vols., Romae, 1921.

Melo, A., *De Exemptione Regularium,* Washington, 1921.

Montalembert, Count de, *Monks of the West,* 5 vols., Boston, 1872.

Mortier, *Histoire des Maitres Generaux de l'Ordre des Freres Precheurs,* 5 vols., 1903-1911.

Mothon, *Institutions Canoniques,* 3 vols., Paris, 1922.

Oesterle, G., *Praelectiones Iuris Canonici,* vol. I, Romae, 1931.

Ojetti, B., *Synopsis Rerum Moralium et Iuris Pontificii,* 3. ed., 4 vols., Romae, 1912.

Ott, Adolf, *Thomas von Aquin und Das Mendikantentum,* Freiburg im Br., Herder, 1908.

Ottaviani, A., *Institutiones Iuris Publici Ecclesiastici,* 2. ed., 2 vols., Romae, 1935-1936.

Papi, Hector, *Religious in Church Law,* New York, 1924.

Pastor, L., *History of the Popes,* 18 vols.; St. Louis, Herder, 1923-1929.

Petra, Vinc., Card., *Commentaria ad Constitutiones Apostolicas,* 5 vols., Venetiis, 1729.

Pejska, J., *Jus Canonicum Religiosorum,* 3. ed., Friburgi Brisgoviae, Herder, 1927.

Pierron, J. B., *Die Katholischen Armen,* Freiburg im Br., Herder, 1911.

Pistocchi, M., *De Bonis Ecclesiae Temporalibus,* Taurini, 1922.

Pruemmer, D., *Manuale Iuris Canonici*, 4. et 5. ed., Friburgi Brisgoviae, Herder, 1927.

Raus, J. B., *Institutiones Canonicae*, 2. ed., Parisiis, Vitte, 1931.

Reiffenstuel, A., *Jus Canonicum Universum*, 5 vols., Antverpiae, 1743.

Rickaby, J., *Moral Philosophy*, 4. ed., London, 1929.

Savigny, F. K., *System des Heutigen Roemischen Rechts*, 8 vols., Berlin, 1840-1849.

Schaefer, T., *Compendium de Religiosis*, Muenster, 1927.

Schmalzgrueber, F., *Ius Ecclesiasticum Universum*, 12 vols., Romae, 1843-1845.

Smith, S. B., *Elements of Ecclesiastical Law*, 3 vols., New York, 1889.

St. Thomas, *Summa Theologica*, Romae, 1886.

Suarez, F., *Opera Omnia*, Parisiis, 1859.

Thomassinus, L., *Vetus et Nova Disciplina Ecclesiae circa Beneficia et Beneficiarios*, Venetiis, 1730.

Vermeersch, A., *Questiones de Justitia*, Brugis, 1901.

Vermeersch, A., *De Religiosis*, 2 vols., Brugis, 1907.

Vermeersch, A.,-Creusen, J., *Epitome Iuris Canonici*, 3. ed., 3 vols., Malines, 1927.

Vromant, G., *De Bonis Ecclesiae Temporalibus*, Louvain, 1934.

Walsh, W. F., *History of English and American Law*, New York, 1923.

Wernz, Fran., *Jus Decretalium*, 2. ed., 6 vols., Romae, 1906-1923.

Whitney, "Religious Movements in the Fourteenth Century," *Cambridge History of English Literature*, vol. II, Cambridge, 1932.

Zollman, Carl, *American Civil Church Law*, 2. ed., St. Paul, Bruce, 1933.

Periodicals

American Ecclesiastical Review, Philadelphia, 1889—.

Apollinaris, Romae, 1928—.

Archiv für Katholisches Kirchenrechts, Mainz, 1857—.

Collationes Brugenses, Brugis, 1896—.

Commentarium pro Religiosis, Romae, 1920—.

Homiletic and Pastoral Monthly, New York, 1900—.

Il Monitore Ecclesiastico, Roma, 1879—.

Ius Pontificium, Romae, 1921—.

Le Canoniste Contemporain, Paris, 1881-1926.

Periodica de re canonica et morali, Brugis, 1905—.

Theologie und Glaube, Paderborn, 1909—.

CHAPTER I

THE RIGHT TO OWN PROPERTY

ARTICLE I. PRELIMINARY NOTIONS

1. MEANING OF PROPERTY.

To express the word 'property' the Code uses the term *bona temporalia*. Though the usual word for property in the *Corpus Juris Romani* is *res*, the word *bona*, probably introduced by Gaius to distinguish praetorian from quiritary ownership,[1] is frequently met with in the writings of the jurists.[2] By *bona*, according to Ulpian, was generally understood a universal inheritance, i. e., not only the assets but also the liabilities of an estate.[3] But more properly, as Iavolenus states, the term is used to designate only the assets, since liabilities can hardly be called *bona*.[4] Apparently it is this second meaning of *bona* that is intended in the Code when mention is made of the property of religious institutes. *Bona temporalia*, then, signify all those things which constitute the wealth or possessions of religious institutes. But it must be kept in mind that 'things' in this sense refer not only to material objects, but also to benefits and rights that are not material but are nevertheless valuable.

2. DIVISION.

The most important classification of property is into *corporeal* property and *incorporeal* property.

---

[1] Leage, *Roman Private Law*, 2. ed., London: Macmillan, 1930, p. 133. Cf. Gaius i.54.

[2] Ulpian—D. (37, 1) 3, pr.; Papinian—D. (16, 2) 16, pr.; Paulus—D. (49, 14) 45, 2; Marcian—D. (35, 3) 8.

[3] D. (37, 1) 3, pr.

[4] "Proprie bona dici non possunt, quae plus incommodi quam commodi habent."—Iavolenus-D. (50, 16) 83.

Corporeal property may be *movable* or *immovable.*

Either corporeal or incorporeal property may be *ecclesiastical,* and if ecclesiastical, also *religious.*

Corporeal and Incorporeal Property.—Those possessions which can be felt or touched, such as land, houses, money, books, etc., are corporeal property. Incorporeal property, on the other hand, is that which has no physical existence, which cannot be touched, and which merely exists in the eye of the law.[5] Thus, the right of way over another's property, or the right to collect a debt, or to receive an inheritance, are not things that can be felt or touched; yet they are rights that have existence before the law, and if they have likewise a money value, they constitute property.[6]

Movable and Immovable Property.—Corporeal property may be either movable or immovable.[7] This division is based on the fundamental distinction which exists between land and things attached to it (immovable goods), and all other property which in its nature is not stationary (movable goods).[8] However, some goods are classified according to the purpose for which they are intended. Money, ordinarily movable property, if destined by a competent superior for the purchase, construction, reparation, etc., of immovable property, is considered as taking the nature of the property for which it is destined and is then immovable property.[9]

---

[5] "Incorporales sunt quae tangi non possunt, qualia sunt ea quae in jure consistunt."—Gaius ii, 14.

[6] Leage, *Roman Private Law,* p. 138.

[7] Rights are incorporeal and cannot be classed as movable or immovable property. Cf. Vromant, *De Bonis Ecclesiae Temporalibus,* 2. ed., Louvain: Museum Lessianum, 1934, p. 36.

[8] Leage, *Roman Private Law,* p. 140.

[9] Schmalzgrueber, *Jus Ecclesiasticum Universum,* 12 vols., Romae, 1843-1845, lib. III, tit. 13, nn. 1, 2, 3; Reiffenstuel, *Jus Canonicum Universum,* 5 vols., Antverpiae, 1743, lib. III, tit. 13, n. 15; Ferraris, *Prompta Bibliotheca Canonica, Juridica, Moralis, Theologica, necnon Ascetica, Polemica, Rubristica, Historica,* 9 vols., Romae, 1885-1892, "alienatio," art. 4, n. 25: Vromant, *De Bonis Ecclesiae Temporalibus,* n. 36.

What if the civil law classification differs from that of the Code? Strictly speaking the Code merely mentions without defining what is movable and what immovable property. Larraona states that in canon law the Roman doctrine of Justinian law regarding movable and immovable goods is received fundamentally. He warns, that as modern codes sometimes extend the Roman law doctrine and receive other divisions which, though similar, are not the same, it will not do to define immovable things by modern codes.[10] Nevertheless, it must be kept in mind that canon 1529 canonizes the civil law formalities for contracts. Therefore if property concerned in a contract has one classification in civil law and another in canon law, the civil law classification should be followed. Even in other cases where contracts are not concerned the civil law classification should be followed if possible, because the spirit of canon 1529 is to avoid friction with the civil law. However, it may not be possible to do this in every case. Thus, in canon law a church building is always immovable property. Yet in civil law, when such a building was put on rollers and moved off the land, it was held to be personal rather than real property.[11]

There are, of course, other ways of classifying property, such as 'precious,' 'sacred,' 'fruitful,' 'consumptible' and their opposites. These will be explained as the need arises.

Ecclesiastical Property.—Either corporeal or incorporeal property can be ecclesiastical. Property is ecclesiastical when it belongs to the Church universal or to an ecclesiastical moral person.[12] By an ecclesiastical moral person is meant a juridical person established by precept of canon law or by formal decree of a competent ecclesiastical superior.[13] Not only churches but also

---

[10] Larraona, "Commentarium Codicis," *Commentarium pro Religiosis,* XIII (1932), 190 note 629.

[11] Beach v. Allen (1876), 7 Hun. (N.Y.) 441. Vromant, *De Bonis Eccl. Temporalibus,* n. 36; De Meester, *Juris Canonici et Juris Canonico-civilis Compendium,* 3 vols., Brugis, 1921-1927, n. 1446.

[12] Canon 1497 § 1.

[13] Canon 100 § 1.

hospitals, asylums, seminaries, parish societies, etc., may be erected into moral persons. When so erected the laws concerning ecclesiastical property are applicable to them whether civil personality has been acquired or not. But the property must already be acquired property, and not merely property to which the moral person has a *jus ad rem*.[14]

Religious Property.—If the ecclesiastical moral person is a religious institute or part of a religious institute the property belonging to it is known as religious ecclesiastical property.[15] Property belonging to individual religious is not religious ecclesiastical property and therefore will not be considered in the pages which follow. It should, however, be noted that there is a class of property which, while not strictly religious property, may be classified as such *quoad administrationem*, and in this case the laws concerning religious property are applicable to it. Thus, the property of individual religious with simple vows[16] is neither ecclesiastical nor religious property. But if a religious (as permitted by canon 569 § 1) ceded the use or usufruct of his or her property to a religious moral person, such property would be religious property *quoad administrationem*.[17] Again, authors are not in agreement concerning the ownership of the dowry prior to the death of the religious, so that it is doubtful whether or not it is religious property.[18] They are, nevertheless, agreed that because of the purpose to which it is destined and because of the right to it which the institute acquires at the death of the religious,[19] it is likened, *quoad administrationem*, to religious ec-

[14] Vromant, *De Bonis Eccl. Temp.*, n. 36.

[15] Larraona, "Commentarium Codicis," *CpR*, XII (1931), 224.

[16] Religious with solemn vows are not allowed to own property.—Can. 581 § 1.

[17] Jansen, *Ordensrecht*, 2. ed., Paderborn: Schoeningh, 1920, p. 273.

[18] Vromant, *De Bonis Eccl. Temp.*, n. 255; Vermeersch-Creusen, *Epitome Juris Canonici*, Brugis, 1924, I, n. 653; Larraona, "Commentarium Codicis," *CpR*, XII (1931), 244; Schaefer, *De Religiosis*, Muenster: Aschendorff, 1927, n. 229.

[19] Canon 548.

clesiastical property.[20] Finally the Friars Minor and the Capuchins because of their renunciation of common property cannot acquire for their order the ownership of any property. The Holy See owns the property acquired by them, and thus, in the strict sense this property is not religious. But because the Holy See grants to the order the use of property and whatever administration is necessitated by this use, the property is, *quoad administrationem,* subject to the special laws for the property of religious.[21]

3. MEANING OF ACQUISITION AND POSSESSION.

The right which is granted to religious moral persons is the right to acquire and possess property. By this is meant the juridical right to obtain and retain the ownership of temporal goods. Though the word *possidere* is used in canon 531, the technical meaning of possession, as distinct from ownership, is not intended, as is clear from canon 1499 § 2.[22] For the rest, as Larraona remarks, *possidere* is very frequently used in the sense of 'to retain.'[23]

Being a juridical right, this ownership may be vindicated in ecclesiastical courts and the competent authority in the ecclesiastical society is obligated to recognize and protect it.[24] Indeed, in strict justice, even the civil authority should recognize and protect this ownership. But except where civil rights are involved this is rarely attended to.

---

[20] The difference of opinion as to ownership of the dowry seems to have no practical bearing. The Code regulates the administration, investment, and final disposition of the dowry. Cf. canons 535 § 2, 549, 550.

[21] Nicholas II, const. *"Exiit qui seminat,"* 14 Aug. 1279—c. 3, *de verborum significatione,* V, 12 in VI°. Clement V, *"Exivi de paradiso,"* 14 May 1312—c. 1, *de verb. sign.,* V, 11 *in Clem.;* Innocent XI, const., *"Solicitudo,"* 20 Nov. 1679—*Monumenta Selecta Juris Regularis,* p. 62, n. 5.

[22] "Dominium bonorum, sub suprema auctoritate Sedis Apostolicae, ad eam pertinet moralem personam, quae eadem bona legitime acquisiverit."—Can. 1499 § 2.

[23] "Commentarium Codicis," *CpR,* XII (1931), 250.

[24] Cf. canons 2346, 2347.

4. PRIVILEGES OF RELIGIOUS PROPERTY.

These privileges do not attach to religious property exclusively, but only in as far as it is ecclesiastical property.

TAX-EXEMPTION.—The Church being a perfect society independent of the State, its property, in theory at least, is not subject to civil tax-laws. This does not mean that church property should not bear its share of the burden of property improvement, nor of other burdens based on commutative justice, nor even that it should refuse to aid civil governments in time of need.[25] But in strict justice the Church is not a subject of taxation for the reason that it is independent of all civil governments. Practically, however, most civil governments consider church property as subject to tax-laws and exemptions of any sort as civil favors. The Church as a matter of prudence and necessity acquiesces.

SPECIAL FORUM.—Because of its connection with spiritual things, litigation concerning ecclesiastical property should be aired in the ecclesiastical court [26] except when a lay person has obtained unjust possession of ecclesiastical property.[27]

PRESCRIPTION.—Sacred things belonging to an ecclesiastical moral person can only be prescribed by another ecclesiastical moral person, not by private individuals.[28]

RESTITUTIO IN INTEGRUM.—The canon law grants to ecclesiastical moral persons the same protection that it grants to minors and wards.[29] An important benefit resulting from this is the

---

[25] Ottaviani, *Institutiones Juris Pub. Eccl.*, I, 400, note 49; II, 182; Vromant, *De Bonis Eccl., Temp.*, n. 9; Wernz, *Jus Decret.*, III, n. 134; Schmalzgrueber, lib. III, tit. 49, c. 3.

[26] Canon 1553 § 1,1°.

[27] Pejska, *Jus Canonicum Religiosorum*, 3. ed., Herder: Friburgi Br., 1927, p. 59.

[28] Canon 1510 § 2. "Dicuntur sacra, quae consecratione vel benedictione ad divinum cultum destinata sunt; . . ."—Can. 1497 § 2.

[29] "Personae morales sive collegiales sive non collegiales minoribus aequiparantur."—Can. 100 § 3.

right to have a negotiation rescinded when it would result in grave injury to the rights of the moral person.[30] This action may be taken even against one's religious superiors who as procurators or administrators have through malice or negligence unjustly alienated the property of the moral person or otherwise caused injury.[31]

5. SOURCES OF LAW.

The specific legislation affecting religious ecclesiastical property is found in the Code under canons 531-537. However, these canons are not the only legislation on the subject. Here and there throughout the Code are found canons which concern the acquisition and administration of religious property.[32] All these canons constitute the *common law* on religious property. To the common law should be added the *particular* law for each institute. This particular law is contained in the rules and constitutions that are not opposed to the common law,[33] in privileges and indults,[34] in legitimate customs,[35] in statutes of superiors and chapters,[36] in special precepts for the institute issued by the Holy See. As a species of particular law may also be mentioned diocesan laws and prescripts. These in so far as they do not conflict with the constitutions, are binding on non-exempt religious, and likewise on exempt religious in matters in which they are subject to the local ordinary.[37]

Directive norms may be gathered from those documents of the Holy See which are not laws in the strict sense, or, if they were laws, have since lost their binding force. Chief among these are:

---

[30] Canon 1687 § 1.

[31] Pejska, *l. c.*

[32] Cf. Canons 580 § 2; 582, 594, 618 § 2,1°, 621, 622, 1495-1551.

[33] Canon 489.

[34] Canon 4.

[35] Canon 25.

[36] Canon 510.

[37] Fanfani, *De Jure Religiosorum* 2. ed., Turin:Marietti, 1925, n. 30.

1. *Normae secundum quas S. Cong. Episcoporum et Regularium procedere solet in approbandis novis institutis votorum simplicium*, 28 June 1901, Romae: Typis S. C. de Propaganda Fide;

2. S. C. de Religiosis, instructio, *Inter ea*, July 30, 1909—*Fontes*, n. 4394.

3. *Normae secundum quas S. Congregatio de Religiosis in novis religiosis congregationibus approbandis procedere solet*, Typis Polyglottis Vaticanis, 1922.

Article II. Historical Outline of the Right to Own Property

1. AFFIRMATION OF THE RIGHT.

Though an outline of the origin of monasteries is not properly a part of the history of administration, still it seems necessary to ask the question whether, in the origin of the monastery, there is anything opposed to the possession of property?

The monastery owes its origin to the hermits.[38] Fearful of denying his faith if subjected to tortures, or of exchanging it for the pleasures of the world, the Christian seeks safety in the desert. At first an effort is made to live in complete solitude. But this mode of life is not without its disadvantages. The hermit may get sick and need assistance; or he cannot bear complete solitude, so he builds his cell near that of another. A third and a fourth join them and they pray together and work together. Perhaps one excels in sanctity or prudence. The others ask his advice. He gives them a rule of life. Others hear of this rule and put it into practice. They come to live near the master; then to live with the master. The time is near the year three hundred. The place is Tabennisi. The first monastery is abuilding.[39]

---

[38] Vermeersch, *De Religiosis Institutis et Personis*, 2. ed., 2 vols., Brugis, 1907, I, n. 41.

[39] Butler, *The Lausiac History of Palladius*, 2 vols., Cambridge, 1898. II, 206.

From this it is apparent that there is nothing in the origin of the monastery that is repugnant to the possession of property. As has been noted, some were urged on by the fear of persecution; others sought to find perfection in prayer and solitude; perhaps even the belief in the *parousia* had not a little to do with determining the religious vocation of some.[40] Individually, it is true, the hermits practiced poverty. But then, neither Paul in his cell nor Simon on his column could have much use for property. And if Anthony, impelled by the *vade et vende* which he heard in the Gospel[41] wooed poverty, it suited the solitary life he had in view. But it must have been a different problem that confronted Pachomius with his thousands of spiritual children looking to him for food and shelter.[42] He needed monasteries; he needed lands; he needed all the means to work the land. As a matter of fact he had these things. The question is by what title did he hold them?

It is not possible, in the early days of the monastery, to base the right to hold property on the law of the Church. In the first place, it must be remembered that the Church was in the midst of a persecution. With Rome incessantly demanding that Jupiter receive his grains of incense, there was little opportunity to be concerned with the property of budding monasteries. Even if external conditions were not adverse, it is doubtful that the Church would have shown much interest at this stage of the monastery's existence. The most that can be said of the monastery is that it was a group of men or women associated for the purposes of religion.[43] It is quite probable that the Church had

---

[40] Grupp, *Kulturgeschichte der roemischen Kaiserzeit*, Muenchen, 1903, I, 455.

[41] Matt. 19:21.

[42] Cf. Bacchus, "Eastern Monasticism," *Catholic Encyclopedia*, X, 464, where it is stated that a Pachomian monastery consisted of about thirty or forty houses with about forty monks in each. Before Pachomius died there were about ten such monasteries.

[43] "Die Orden hatten in ihren Anfängen gar night die bewuszte Tendenz, sich zu besondern Organen der kirchlichen Regierung oder Mission zu

already taken cognizance of the existence of monasteries; but not that they had been recognized or approved as organizations within the Church coming under the scope of her legislation.

ROMAN LAW.—The civil law of Rome does not answer the question any better if merely the beginning of the monastery is considered. It is quite probable that in time of peace under the Roman Law Christians were allowed to hold property.[44] But it must be remembered that an important factor in the rise of the monastery was not peace but persecution. That monasteries had any civilly valid titles to property, is hard to imagine in view of the fact that even private individuals were deprived of their property for the mere fact of being Christians. Under the circumstances it is probable that the desert, which had already offered protection against anti-christian laws, was again relied upon to protect the property of the monastery. Thus, the title by which the monasteries possessed their property was, in the beginning, the Law of Nature, always a valid title when positive laws are silent or adverse.[45]

Valid titles, however, are of little use to the weak when the will to take possesses the strong. For this reason it is unthinkable that monasteries could have increased their property holdings to any great extent, or continued in the possession of them for any length of time if civil laws remained opposed to the principles for which monasteries existed. Fortunately, however, for Religion, the Cross which brought victory at the Milvian

---

gestalten. . . . Ihre Absicht ging ganz und gar auf das innerliche Opfer zum Zwecke eines Lebens der Vollkommenheit in der Nachfolge Christi."—Linsenmann, *Denkschrift über die Frage der Männerorden in Württemberg*, Stuttgart, 1892, p. 51.

[44] Doheny, *Church Property, Modes of Acquisition*, Canon Law Studies, n. 41, Wash., Catholic University of America, 1927, p. 16.

[45] Some deny that the Law of Nature gives anyone a right to property. For a defense of the opinion, cf. *Summa* II-II Q. LXVI; De Lugo, *Disputationes Scholasticae et Morales*, 9. ed., Parisiis, 1869, disputatio 6, "De Justitia et Jure"; Vermeersch, *Questiones de Justitia*, Brugis, 1901, p. 187. Vromant, *De Bonis Ecclesiae Temporalibus*, n. 3.

Bridge [46] won a place in the esteem of the Roman General; and thereafter, the Followers of the Cross could practice their religion with perfect freedom. By the Edict of Milan (313) and by subsequent legislation of Constantine [47] the Catholic Church received not only the legal right to acquire new property by legitimate means, but also special favors and a return of the property of which it had been formerly despoiled.[48]

Naturally, the force of this edict was felt in the Roman provinces of Africa, and the favor of the civil law was a great aid to the growth of the monasteries. Thus, though the monastery owes its existence in part to the adverse character of the laws of Rome, its growth and development are due in a large measure to the toleration and favor of these same laws. In general, however, the condition of the monastery follows the condition of the Church itself. For while the monasteries profited from the changed attitude of Rome towards the Catholic Church, the change came about without any special reference to the monasteries as such. The first law that refers explicitly to the

[46] "There will never be agreement whether or not an objective miracle was performed by God to procure Constantine's conversion—never at least until the outlook on the universe of all men becomes identical."—Baynes, *Constantine the Great and the Christian Church, British* Academy: London, 1929, p. 58, note 32. (The authors on each side of the discussion are cited in the same footnote.)

[47] "In February 313, Licinius met Constantine at Milan, and there married Constantine's sister. At this meeting a policy of complete religious freedom was agreed upon. The corporation of the Christian Church—or rather, perhaps, of each separate Christian Church—was recognized as a legal person; the text was doubtless settled of a rescript which would be put into force by Licinius on his return to the East. It is that text which is generally known as the Edict of Milan. Seeck has shown that we cannot prove that there ever was an edict issued, but this is so because in all probability Constantine had anticipated the agreement in policy reached at Milan in rescripts similar to that directed to Anullinus, which had been sent to all the governors of the Western provinces. The Edict of Milan may be a fiction, but the fact for which the term stood remains untouched." —Baynes, *Constantine the Great and the Christian Church*, p. 11.

[48] Eusebius, *Historia Ecclesiastica*, X, 5—*MPG*, XX, 879.

monks is a law of the year 390. This law interdicted the cities and towns to the monks, and ordered them to confine themselves to the deserts.[49] This constitution implicitly gives testimony to the growing numbers of the monks and from these numbers we can argue to the possession of lands and monasteries even though still located in *loca deserta.* There is no law that expressly gives to monasteries the right to hold property. But in view of the general edict of toleration, no such law was necessary. As groups associated for the purposes of religion, the monks had the right to hold property. This right is indicated by a law which speaks of dividing the property of monasteries *pro rata* when a separation was ordered between the male and female members of the so-called 'double monasteries.'[50] Very probably too, the monks felt they could be beneficiaries under the law which said: "*Habeat unusquisque licentiam sanctissimo catholicae venerabilique concilio decedens bonorum quod optavit relinquere.*"[51] Indeed, like the Church itself the property of the monastery received special protection. Thus, in the matter of legacies and inheritances, we find this law in the Code: "*Sancimus res ad venerabiles ecclesias . . . vel monasteria . . . lucrativorum inscriptionibus liberas immunesque esse.*"[52]

As to the administrators and mode of administration of the temporal goods of monasteries, the Roman Law while not minute, has sufficient detail. But in this Justinian pretends merely to patronize conciliar legislation of the Church. "*Sancimus igitur sacros canones secuti*";[53] a statement which he softened later on to: "*Sequimur enim divinos canones et sanctissimos patres.*"[54]

Details concerning the acts of temporal administration are omitted. But the monks generally are forbidden to leave their

---

[49] "Quicumque sub professione monachi repperiuntur, deserta loca et vastas solitudines sequi adque habitare iubeantur."—Codex Theod. (16, 3) 1.

[50] C. (1, 3) 43, 4; N. (123, 36).

[51] C. (1, 2).

[52] C. (1, 2) 22, pr.

[53] N. (5, 2) pr.

[54] N. 133 pr.

monasteries, even for the purpose of transacting their business. This is to be attended to by their agents.[55] Whether or not these agents had to be monks is not evident; though it appears from another law that they could be. But in this case the law prescribed that they be old monks, not easily corrupted.[56] The agents were of special importance in conducting the affairs of nuns.[57]

Schaefer, in an article on Justinian and the Monastic life, says that it was the high regard in which Justinian held the monastic life that dictated the disciplinary measures which he promulgated, and that in this his efforts are worthy of admiration, esteem, and thanks. At the same time he points out that Justinian in this legislation, even while he worked to the advantage of the monastery, exceeded his competency.[58]

CHURCH LAW: MONASTIC DEVELOPMENT.—Before the fourth century had run its course the monasteries appear in Italy, Spain, France, Ireland and Africa.[59] In proportion to the increase of monasteries is the increase in the number of monks. However, this rapid growth is not without difficulties. In the early days of monasticism perseverance in the religious life was not thought to be the most serious of obligations.[60] Whatever the 'practice' may have been, there was usually no 'profession' of vows as it is understood now.[61] Even perseverance in any one monastery was not always the custom.[62] Under the circumstances it is easy to imagine that abuses could and did arise. The Council at Chalcedon in 451 passed legislation to remedy

---

[55] N. (123, 42).

[56] N. (133, 5).

[57] N. (133, 5).

[58] Schaefer, "Justinianus et Vita Monastica," *Acta Congressus Juridici Internationalis,* I, 176 ff.

[59] Vermeersch, *De Religiosis,* II, 8.

[60] The obligation to persevere was sanctioned by the II Council of Arles (452), can. 25—Harduin, II, 775.

[61] Vermeersch, *De Religiosis,* I, 30.

[62] C. of Chalcedon (451), can. 4—Harduin, II, 602.

prevailing abuses. Thereafter no monastery could be erected without the bishop's consent, and the monks, at least in what concerns external activities, were subject to his power.[63] But later councils narrowed somewhat the limits of episcopal power. The Third Council of Arles in 455, and the Councils of Carthage of 525 and 534, reserved the government of the monastery to the abbot, allowing to the bishop only the ordination of clerics and the dedication of oratories.[64] As to temporal goods, little can be said with definiteness or exactness. There is much confusion and much that is obscure. Most difficult of all to determine is the exact person or persons in whom the title of ownership was vested. It may have been the diocese, or the monastery, or the associated monks, or the abbot, or the poor, or the titular saint. All these have been suggested by the authors; but the legislation is not definite.[65]

St. Benedict.—This state of affairs lasted till the Rule of St. Benedict started a new era in monastic life.[66] Writing on the "Rule of St. Benedict," G. Cyprian Alston says that this rule holds first place among monastic legislative codes and was the most important factor in the organization and spread of monasticism in the West.[67] It is this factor of better organization that clears up in a large measure the problem of temporal goods. Henceforth the rule is fixed and permanent and no one is allowed to change it. The monk is expected to persevere not only in the religious life, but in the very monastery he has chosen. He is now a member of a family. He possesses nothing of his own. Even the fruits of his personal labor go to the com-

---

[63] *Ibid.* cc. 4, 8.

[64] III C. of Arles (455)—Harduin, II, 781; C. of Carthage (525)—Harduin, II, 1087; C. of Carthage (534)—Harduin, II, 1177. (A fuller consideration of these councils is given in chapter II of this outline.)

[65] Doheny, *Church Property*, p. 19.

[66] Note: The purpose of St. Basil was similar to that of St. Benedict, but his influence was confined chiefly to the East.

[67] Catholic Encycl. II, 436.

munity.[68] Under such a system it is natural that the monastery's temporal possessions increased greatly. This was in accord with the ideas of St. Benedict. He did not, to be sure, desire an increase of possessions in order to promote the comfort and ease of his spiritual sons, but he did believe them necessary to further the work and usefulness of his communities. He did not intend that his sons should ask alms, but that they should give them; that they should relieve the poor, clothe the naked, help the afflicted, entertain travellers, etc.[69] Other chapters in the Rule of St. Benedict confirm the view that he pre-supposed the possession of temporal goods by the monasteries. Thus in cc. 31 and 32 he orders the appointment of cellarers and other officials, that they may care for the 'goods' of the monastery. In c. 33 it is stated that the abbot is to supply what is needed by the subjects. Chapter 57 has regulations about the sale of what the monastery possesses.[70]

These facts do not take on any special importance merely because they are in the Rule of St. Benedict. But they do become significant, when it is recalled that the Rule of St. Benedict became the model rule for religious institutes and was almost universally followed from the eighth to the twelfth century;[71] that at a period when general councils were unknown in the West, national and provincial councils ordered all religious to follow the Rule of St. Benedict,[72] in this way identifying the Rule of St. Benedict with ecclesiastical legislation. Dudden in his work on St. Gregory the Great states that it is evident from the writings and legislation of this pontiff that he approved what-

---

[68] St. Benedict expected his monks to work five hours daily. Cf. Logeman, *Rule of St. Benet*, London, 1888, p. 81.

[69] Ford, "St. Benedict," *Cath. Encycl.*, II, 436.

[70] Logeman, *Rule of St. Benet*, pp. 61-64, 94.

[71] Vermeersch, *De Religiosis*, I, 33.

[72] C. of Artun (670), c. 15—*MPL*, LXVI, 213; C. of Frankfort (802), c. 23—Hefele, *Conciliengeschichte*, III, 744.

ever St. Benedict wrote in his Rule concerning the administration of the property of religious.[73]

Later Church Law.—Laws of St. Gregory establish the right of religious institutes to the ownership of property, and these laws constitute the basis of present day canon law. Thus, writing to the subdeacon Gratiosus, Pope Gregory commands him to give some property belonging to the Church as a donation to a certain Abbess Flora, that she may use it for a monastery.[74] He commands that it be given "*proprietatis jure procul dubio possidendam.*" In another letter to Marinianus, Bishop of Ravenna, he exhorts him to confirm the donations which one of his predecessors had made to a certain monastery.[75] In a letter to the subdeacon Peter, he orders him not to act against the property rights of a certain monastery, if they can prove that they have been in peaceful possession of the property for forty years, thus acknowledging the right of religious institutes to acquire property by prescription.[76]

From these words of St. Gregory, who ruled the Church from 590-604, it is seen that at this early date the right of religious institutes to the ownership of property had received recognition from the supreme authority in the Church. That this right was proper to the institute and not subject to the right of the local ordinary, or the civil power is evident from later legislation. Thus, the Fourth Council of Toledo (671) states that the only rights granted to the bishops over monks are:

> Monachos ad conversationem sanctam praemonere, abbates aliaque officia instituere, atque extra regulam acta corrigere. . . . Quod si (episcopi) aliquid in monachis (*sic*) canonibus interdictum praesumpserint aut usurpare quidpiam de monasterii rebus tentaverint, non

[73] Dudden, *St. Gregory the Great, His Place in History and Thought,* London, 1905, I, 79.

[74] C. 75, C. XII, q. 2.

[75] C. 3, C. XII, q. 5.

[76] C. 2, C. XVI, q. 4.

> deerit ab illis sententia excommunicationis qui se deinceps nequaquam substulerint ab illicitis.[77]

The Council of Mainz (796) decreed that the local bishop could not take away the temporal possessions of a monastery because of the misconduct of the abbot.[78] The implication of this decree is that at this time the goods of a monastery were considered as belonging to the monastery or associated members and not to the superior or local ordinary.

In the year 1199 Pope Innocent III ordered that certain possessions taken from a monastery should be restored to that monastery even though the method of taking them was strictly in accord with the civil law. The pontiff in this case asserted that the civil law had no power over church goods unless the law had been approved by the Church.[79] Again in a letter to the Archbishop of Lyons, the same pontiff declared that property given to pious places rightfully belonged to those places even though the donation was according to popular custom and not according to the strict precept of civil law.[80]

By the beginning of the thirteenth century, then, it is well established ecclesiastical law that religious institutes have the right to acquire and possess temporal goods in the various legitimate ways. It is evident that this right is not dependent on the will of the bishop and still less on the will of the civil government. Though there is no certain evidence that religious institutes have received formal approbation as yet, still it is clear that they have been taken under the protection of the Church and have been made participators of her right as a perfect society to possess what is needful.

LATER CIVIL LAW.—As to the attitude of the Civil Law towards the acquisition of property by religious institutes during this period, the conclusion seems inevitable, that only on the

---

[77] IV C. of Toledo (671), c. 51—*MPL*, LXXXIV, 378.

[78] C. 7, C. XVI, q. 6.

[79] C. 10, X, *de constitutionibus*, I, 2.

[80] C. 2, X, *de consuetudine*, I, 4.

grounds that it was favorable is it possible to explain the rapid growth in wealth and members of the monasteries. In the fifth. sixth and seventh centuries, France, Spain, England, Italy and Germany enter the fold of the True Church. Emperors become Christians. Christianity becomes the only religion of the State. Thus, the growth of the Church aids the growth of the monastery and the new faith stirs princes and people to deeds of generosity in favor of religion.[81] About the same time the feudal system and rural parishes came into vogue. Each petty prince had his church or system of churches, and in many cases the monks were invited to care for them and to establish schools. Infant baptism became the rule and undoubtedly increased the possible number of candidates for the religious life.[82]

In the eighth, ninth and tenth centuries, besides the conversion to Christianity of the Swedes and Norwegians, the Russians and Poles, there is seen the rise and rapid spread of the temporal power of the Popes. Perhaps this more than any other single factor accounts for the favor shown to monks and monasteries in this period. The power that could make a Henry come to Canossa undoubtedly could command respect for religious persons and places. But in particular with regard to religious institutes, one has only to scan the roster of those who were members of the monasteries in some way or other, to see the weight of influence that was enjoyed by the monasteries at both temporal and spiritual courts. In the institute of St. Benedict alone, from its foundation to the year 1300, it is said that among its members were numbered twenty-four popes, two hundred cardinals, seven thousand archbishops, fifteen thousand bishops, twenty emperors, ten empresses, forty-seven kings and fifty queens.[83] If this be true it is a guarantee that civil laws in this period were favorable to the material growth of the monas-

[81] *Capitularium Regum Francorum,* tom. 1, col. 406; tom. 2, col. 109.

[82] Kirch, *Enchiridion Fontium Historiae Antiquae,* 4. ed., Freiburg: Herder, 1923, p. 907.

[83] Alston, "Benedictine Order," *Cath. Encycl.,* II, 446.

teries in spite of any shadows cast by the efforts of individual princes and patrons to domineer the Church and control her revenues.

2. RESTRICTION OF THE RIGHT.

Rise of the Mendicant Orders.—It was seen in the preceding pages how prior to the thirteenth century, the right of religious institutes to the ownership of property was clearly established in Church Law, and was unquestioned in Civil Law; unquestioned, i. e., if one is content to look upon the depredations of feudal barons as an abuse of power rather than a denial of right. The extent to which this right could be exercised seems in many cases to have been unlimited; with the result, that the wealth of some monasteries grew out of all proportion to the needs of the members or of their activities. Consequent upon the increase of temporal goods were relaxation and slackening of religious zeal and discipline. The people were neglected not only by the monks but by all branches of the clergy; and being quick to sense the root of the evil cried out against clerical wealth.[84]

It must have occurred to many that a remedy for the evils lay in the renunciation or at least in the sparing use of temporal goods; and this probably explains the welcome accorded the doctrines of Peter Waldo. But unfortunately, for lack of direction, the Waldenses lapsed into error and were condemned by the Church.[85] Better fortune, however, followed the footsteps of Francis of Assisi. And though it probably cannot be proved that the 'Umbrian Poverello' had at the outset any other intention but that of his own spiritual perfection, still the movement that he started did, in fact, very much to remedy the evils of the

---

[84] Cf. Pope Innocent III, "Epistolae"—*MPL,* CCXV, CCXVI; Koch, *Graf Elger vom Holmstein,* p. 70-72; Pierron, *Die Katholischen Armen,* p. 99. Ott, *Thomas von Aquin und Das Mendikantentum,* p. 47; Felder, *Ideals of St. Francis,* pp. 94-96.

[85] Pope Lucius III, decretum *"Ad abolendam,"* 1181—Mansi, XXII, 476.

times and to restore the confidence of the people in their spiritual leaders.[86]

The characteristic note of the Franciscan movement[87] was the absolute renunciation of all right to ownership of property.[88] It has been seen that in the religious institutes of the past the members renounced the individual right to the ownership of property. In the Franciscan institutes, as in the Dominican and other mendicant orders which followed the lead of St. Francis,[89] not only individual property, but even the right to own property for the common needs, was renounced by the members. The ideal proposed by the Saint of Assisi was that members of his institute should renounce all worldly things for the service of God, depending only on the alms and charity of the faithful.[90]

Ecclesiastical Approbation of Absolute Poverty.—In the year 1209 St. Francis asked the Holy See for approval of his institute, but his request was at first denied. Historians tell us,

[86] "When the Church was in danger of losing the hearts of the people, the mendicant friars made her again popular."—Koch, *Die frühesten Niederlassung der Minoriten im Rheingebiete*, p. 113; Ott, *Thomas von Aquin und Das Mendikantentum*, p. 50.

[87] Note: The emphasis in this section will be on the Franciscan Order for the reason that most of the legislation dealing with the exclusion of the right to property is connected with this Order.

[88] *Rule of St. Francis*, c. 6.

[89] In the sense that St. Francis was the first to make absolute poverty a rule for his order. As to whether or not St. Francis was imitated by St. Dominic and others, cf. Guiraud, *Questions*, "St. Dominique," p. 153; Sabatier, *Vie de St. Francois*, p. 251.—Perhaps this statementt of Pierron, is nearest the truth: "Und wenn man tatsächlich einen Einflusz geltend machen will, so ist derselbe nicht so sehr bei Franziskus als beim Heiligen Stuhle selbst zu suchen. Nicht Franziskus, sondern der Heilige Stuhl war das leitende Motiv in der Entwicklung der beiden religiösen Orden zu reinen Bettelorden."—*Die Katholischen Armen*, p. 140.

[90] "Fratres nihil sibi approprient, nec domum, nec locum, nec aliquam rem: sed tamquam peregrini et advenae in hoc saeculo in paupertate et humilitate Domino famulantes, vadant pro eleemosyna confidenter."—Regula, c. 6.

however, that Pope Innocent III, after refusing this request, saw in a dream a tottering Lateran Basilica, which would have fallen except for the support given it by St. Francis. He thereupon recalled the Saint and gave verbal approbation of the institute. In the year 1223, the rule, re-written by St. Francis, received formal approbation from Pope Honorius III.[91]

Thus, it would seem that the year 1209 is the starting point for the legislation found in the Code of Canon Law, which admits of limitations or even exclusion of the right to hold property in certain religious institutes.[92] However, it must not be supposed from this legislation that the Church denies to any institute the right to the ownership of property. Canon 531 is clear in stating that not only the institute but the province and the house have the right to acquire and possess temporal goods. But where an institute has established as an ideal for its members the complete or partial renunciation of this right, the Church in approving such an institute insists that for the future the members faithfully observe this renunciation which has become for them a particular law.

Opposition to This Ideal.—It cannot be said that this ideal of St. Francis encountered no opposition whatever. Even in the lifetime of St. Francis, probably because of the increased numbers of his followers, efforts were made to relax somewhat the severity of his law on poverty.[93] The Saint found it necessary in his 'Testament' to insist on the literal observance of his rule, especially with regard to poverty. After his death (1226), continuous efforts were made to have the rule changed, and not a few were of the opinion that its observance was illicit and harmful, if not the next thing to suicide.[94]

---

[91] Bulla, *"Solet annuere,"* 29 Nov. 1223—*Bull. Franc.*, I, 15.

[92] Canon 531.

[93] Balthasar, *Geschichte des Armutsstreites im Franziskanerorden*, pp. 9, 27.

[94] Nicholas III, bull. *"Exiit qui seminat,"* 14 Aug. 1279—c. 3, *de verb. sign*,, V, 12 in Sexto.

Ecclesiastical Legislation on Absolute Poverty.—Though the incidents already mentioned are not legislation, they give the background for the legislation which followed.

As has been seen, the Rule of St. Francis received verbal approbation from Innocent III in 1209, and formal approbation from Honorius III in 1223. In the year 1230 Pope Gregory IX declared that the 'last testament' which St. Francis had written at Cortona in 1226 had no binding force on the members.[95] As a matter of fact, the Pope interpreted the rule to the extent of allowing the general or provincial superiors to employ a messenger (*nuntius*) or syndic to receive and expend money for the immediate necessities of the friars, and permitted them the use of furniture, books, and other movables (though it was not made clear to whom these goods strictly speaking belonged), and of houses and places which remained the property of the donors. The declaration of Innocent IV in 1245 went further, as it permitted recourse to the messenger or syndic not only for necessities but also for the convenience of the brethren, and made the Holy See the owner of the lands, houses, and goods used by the friars, where ownership was not expressly reserved to the donors.[96] This privilege was renounced by the friars themselves a few years later in 1249.[97]

But the agitation in favor of a relaxation of poverty did not cease. In 1279, at the instance of the commissarius generalis, Bonagratia, a committee of friars petitioned Pope Nicholas III, for a definition of the rule. Against those who considered the absolute renunciation of property as illicit and unobservable, Pope Nicholas declared that if done out of love for God it was meritorious and holy. The Pope then distinguished between the ownership, possession, usufruct, right to use, and the simple fact

[95] Bulla, *"Quo elongati,"* 1230—*Bull. Franc.*, I, 68.

[96] Innocent IX, bull. *"Ordinem vestrum,"* 14 Nov. 1245—*Bull. Franc.*, I, 400; *Cambridge Medieval History*, VI, 733; Oliger, "Rule of St. Francis," *Cath. Encycl.*, VI, 212; Ilg, *Explanation of the Rule of the Friars Minor*, p. 168; *Constitutiones Generales O. F. M.*, (1922), n. 239.

[97] *Analecta Franciscana*, I, 285.

of using property, declaring that the friars were allowed the use of temporal goods but had not the right to use them (*jus utendi*); and moreover, that the ownership (*dominium*) of these things was vested in the Holy See.[98]

From about the year 1290, a contention had arisen as to whether the Franciscan vow of poverty restricted only the ownership of property or both ownership and use. This eventually led in 1310-1312, to the '*Magna Disputatio*' at Avignon, which was settled by Pope Clement V, who at the Council of Vienne (1313) issued his famous constitution "*Exivi de paradiso.*" By this declaration the renunciation of property was retained; the friars were allowed only the use of the goods given them, and where the rule prescribed it, only the restricted use (*usus pauper*).[99]

It would seem that after so many papal declarations favoring absolute poverty for certain religious institutes the question could no longer be a matter for controversy. However, discussions continued, especially the theoretical one between the Franciscans and Dominicans of 1321, which led in the following year to a complete reversal of ecclesiastical legislation on absolute poverty by Pope John XXII. Declaring that the law which reserved the ownership of property to the Pope and the Holy See was more a disadvantage than a help to the friars in removing solicitude for temporal things; and that it was contrary to law and reason to say that the use of consumptible things could be separated from the ownership of them, Pope John decreed that henceforth the ownership of such things did not belong to the Holy See but to the friars themselves.[100]

However, as the Popes Honorius III, Gregory IX, Innocent IV, Alexander IV, and Nicholas IV, had approved the Rule of St. Francis and its precept of absolute poverty, a question was

---

[98] Nicholas III, const. "*Exiit qui seminat,*" 14 Aug. 1279—c. 3, *de verborum significatione*, V, 12 in Sexto.

[99] C. 1, *de verborum significatione*, V, 11 in Clem.

[100] John XXII, const. "*Ad conditorem canonum,*" 8 Dec. 1322—c. 3, *de verborum significatione*, tit. XIV in Extrav. Joan. XXII.

raised by many as to the right of the Pope to change the laws of his predecessors. But Pope John maintained his right and reaffirmed his constitution of 1325.[101]

Thus, for one hundred years the absolute renunciation of property was forbidden by the Church. However, in 1428 Pope Martin V, in his constitution "*Amabiles fructus*" abrogated the law of Pope John XXII, and the Franciscans de observantia were once again allowed to practice absolute renunciation of temporal goods.[102]

At the Council of Trent the right to practice absolute poverty was defended by the General, Francisco Zamora, and though the Council decreed that henceforth "real property (*bona immobilia*) may be possessed by all monasteries and houses, both of men and women, and of mendicants, even by those who were forbidden by their constitutions to possess it, or who had not received permission to that effect by apostolic privilege," yet permission was given to the Minor Observants and the Capuchins to follow the rule of absolute poverty prescribed by St. Francis.[103]

The introduction of institutes of simple vows into the life of the Church has necessitated no greater change in this legislation than the extension of capacity to provinces and houses. According to Larraona, the Code presumes the existence of this capacity not only in the institute, but also in provinces and houses, so that its non-existence would have to be demonstrated.[104]

Present State of Affairs.—At present, then, the only institutes practicing absolute poverty in its fullest sense are the first orders of the Friars Minor and the Capuchins. A decree of the Sacred Congregation of the Council said it was the opinion of the Sacred Congregation that the Second Order of Franciscans (Poor Clares), was not included in the exception to the decree

---

[101] *Ibidem.*

[102] *Bullarium Franciscanum,* VII, 712.

[103] C. of Trent, Sess. XXV, *de reg.*, c. 3.

[104] "Commentarium Codicis," *CpR,* XII (1931), 353.

of the Council of Trent made in favor of the Friars Minor and the Capuchins.[105]

The Order of Preachers when founded by St. Dominic did not have the practice of absolute poverty. However, at the Chapter of 1220, they relinquished all possessions and revenues and adopted the practice of strict poverty.[106] This practice Pope Benedict XII, tried to restrict but without success. However, in 1475 the Order petitioned Pope Sixtus IV for the right to hold property and this was granted.[107]

Independent houses and houses of the professed of the Society of Jesus are not allowed to have any real property besides a dwelling, a church and a garden.[108] The constitutions of the Carmelites state that houses are not allowed to have revenues without the consent of the General Definitors.[109] But it would seem that these must be classed as restrictions upon the houses of the institute rather than upon the institute itself. The same restrictions may be in force in recently established congregations.

Absolute Poverty and the Civil Law.—As regards this feature of the temporal goods of religious institutes and the civil law, there is, of course, no difficulty. It is the possession of goods not the renunciation of them that leads to civil legislation. Moreover, in this period the civil law for clerics was administered in ecclesiastical courts, and in such cases the norm followed was the law of the Church.

3. NEGATION OF THE RIGHT.

Fourth to Fourteenth Century.—When the monasteries came into existence at the end of the third century, the condition

---

[105] *Severini,* July 1587—*Fontes,* n. 2183. One family of Poor Clares retains the privilege of absolute poverty granted three days before the death of Clare.

[106] Denifle, *Archiv,* I, 212; Pierron, *Die Katholischen Armen,* p. 139.

[107] Mortier, *Histoire des Maitres Generaux de l'Ordres des Freres Precheurs,* IV, 495; *Cambridge Medieval History,* VI, 741

[108] Vermeersch, *De Religiosis,* I, 38.

[109] *Constitutiones O.C.D.,* pars. I, c. 3, n. 1.

of civil affairs placed not only their property holdings but their very existence in a precarious condition. The edict of Milan, however, gave the Church and the monasteries a civil standing that enabled them to possess their property in peace.[110] From this time till the fourteenth century, it seems quite correct to say that the temporal affairs of the monasteries grew increasingly better. Later laws of Constantine and his successors, especially the Emperor Justinian, not only opened to the religious houses all those modes of acquisition which were allowed to others, but surrounded them with special protective laws and also granted privileges and immunities which increased still more their holdings.[111] While the feudal system, in many cases, obliged the monastery to the payment of a tax in lieu of services to the lord, yet it made possible grants of land from the lords to the monasteries which amply compensated for the tax. The increase of the temporal power of the Popes is an important factor in explaining the increased wealth of the monasteries. Ecclesiastical government upheld the right of the monasteries to temporal goods and civil governments, in many instances, lacked the power to withdraw it. Undoubtedly, during these years, there were murmurings from time to time against the wealth of the clergy and especially of the religious.[112] The Waldenses of the twelfth and thirteenth centuries have already been mentioned; and in a sense the Mendicant Movement was a protest against clerical wealth. But the first serious rumblings were not heard until the fourteenth century and strangely enough the friars were the occasion.

FOURTEENTH TO TWENTIETH CENTURY: DOCTRINAL NEGATION. —About the middle of the fourteenth century a controversy was

---

[110] "Edictum Constantini Magni pro Religionis Libertate"—*MPL*, VIII, 106.

[111] N. 83; 131.

[112] "Die vereinte Laieninitiative hatte vor allem eine ausgesprochen religiöse Tendenz und war nicht gegen die Kirche als solche, sondern hauptsächlich gegen die Prunksucht und den Reichtum des Klerus."—Pierron, *Die Katholischen Armen*, p. 2.

waging in England between the mendicants and the secular clergy. Richard Fitz-Ralph, Archbishop of Armagh, and one time chancellor of Oxford (1333), took up the defense of the secular clergy. He attacked the mendicant ideal of poverty and introduced an idea of ownership which made it depend on grace. Those in the state of grace had a right to property; those in sin had forfeited this right.[113] Though Fitz-Ralph kept his arguments within the sphere of the theoretical and ideal, John Wyclif, a contemporary, lost no time in urging their practical application. By means of his 'poor priests'[114] he spread abroad the doctrine that the property of anyone in mortal sin did not have to be respected. He even went further than the argument authorized, for he came to hold that no monk or clerk, not even the righteous, could hold temporal possessions without sin; that it was lawful for kings and princes to deprive the religious of what was held unlawfully.[115]

The outcome of Wyclif's doctrine was not only the Lollard Heresy with its consequent pillaging of churches and monasteries; but by means of itinerant scholars it passed from England to Bohemia and Moravia, where it was taken up by John Huss and resulted in the Hussite Heresy and the Hussite Wars.[116] In these wars besides the despoiling of many churches and convents, the Catholics suffered several severe defeats. Article three of the Four Articles of Prague, which were submittd by the heretics as a basis for peace, reads as follows:

> The priests and monks, of whom many meddle with the affairs of the State, are to be deprived of the worldly goods which they possess in great quantities, and which make them neglect their sacred office, and their goods shall be restored to us, in order that, in accordance with the doctrine of the Gospel, and the practice of the

[113] Whitney, "Religious Movements in the Fourteenth Century," *Cambridge History of English Literature,* II, 52.

[114] The poor priests were laymen imbued with the doctrines of Wyclif.

[115] Pastor, *History of the Popes,* I, 160.

[116] *Ibid.* p. 161.

Apostles, the clergy shall be subject to us, and, living in poverty, serve as a pattern of humility to others.[117]

In his constitution of February 22, 1418, Pope Martin V declared the doctrines of Wyclif and Huss "sacrilegious, false and pernicious" and among others condemned:

> Art. 10.—It is contrary to Sacred Scripture, that ecclesiastics should have possessions.
>
> Art. 16.—Temporal rulers can arbitrarily take temporal goods from the Church if the ones possessing them are habitually delinquent.
>
> Art. 18.—Tithes are purely alms, and parishoners can, because of the sins of their pastors, seize them at will.
>
> Art. 32.—To enrich the clergy is contrary to the law of Christ.
>
> Art. 34.—All mendicants are heretics; and those who give them alms are excommunicated.
>
> Art. 39.—The emperor and secular lords are seduced by the devil when they endow the Church with temporal goods.
>
> Art. 44.—Augustine, Benedict and Bernard have been damned, unless they have repented of the fact that they had possessions and established and entered religious institutes; and so from the Pope to the last religious, all are heretics.[118]

THE REFORMATION.—Following upon the heresies of Wyclif and Huss one finds next, in the question of temporal goods, the Protestant 'Reformation' and its policy of spoliation. It would perhaps be hard to prove a direct connection between the heresies of Wyclif and Huss and the Reformation. But there can be no doubt that the doctrines on property of these heresiarchs were still alive at the time of the Reformation and had their sinister influence on the conduct of the reformers towards religious insti-

---

[117] Wilhelm, "Huss and the Hussites," *Cath Encycl.*, VII, 587.

[118] Martin V, const. *"Inter cunctas,"* Feb. 22, 1418, par. 11—*Fontes*, n. 43.

tutes. Though there is no ecclesiastical legislation directly applicable to this phase of the Reformation, the Council of Trent reiterates the now well-established law relative to the right of religious institutes to acquire and possess property. With the exception of the Friars Minor and the Capuchins, even those who were formerly mendicants are for the future allowed to acquire property.[119]

Political Negation.—The eighteenth century gave birth to a type of statesman that was distinctly anti-clerical and inimical to the rights and immunities of the Church and of religious institutes. The names of Tanucci, Pombal, Choiseul and Aranda need but be mentioned to conjure up a whole series of concerted efforts to make the Church the puppet of the State and to strip it of every right and privilege.

Under the influence of Tanucci laws were passed in Parma and Piacenza in 1764, by which no one was allowed to donate to the Church any land or money in excess of three hundred dollars. Even this amount, if it represented more than one-twentieth of one's total estate, was forbidden. All those who made religious profession were obliged to renounce their civil right to hold property. Failing in this they were penalized with the loss of civil personality. All Church property was declared subject to taxation and the law decreeing this was made retroactive for two hundred years.

After much effort Pope Clement XIII succeeded in obtaining a recognition of the Church's right to acquire real property; but in 1767, greater restrictions were placed upon the rights of the Church. A civil magistrate was placed in charge of ecclesiastical property and institutes and allowed to regulate dowries, legacies and applications to religious institutes. These magistrates even went so far as to make decisions concerning the celebration of Mass and the administration of the Sacraments. To all these abuses Clement XIII replied by excommunicating Tanucci and

---

[119] C. of Trent, Sess. XXV, *de regul.*, c. 3.

re-affirming the rights of the Church and religious institutes by declaring all these iniquitous laws null and void.[120]

A policy similar to that of Tanucci was inaugurated by Pombal in Portugal. This statesman directed his main efforts against the Society of Jesus. In 1759 their property was sequestered, and in the following year they themselves were expelled from the country. After unsuccessful efforts to have Pope Clement XIII suppress the Society, Pombal who had made himself the "effective head" of the Church in Portugal gained his point with the succeeding Pope, Clement XIV, who to avoid a schism suppressed the Society in 1773.[121]

In France, Choiseul engineered the "Family Compact" of the Bourbons, which Goyau calls "the greatest effort of lay absolutism against ecclesiastical autonomy and vitality."[122] The Jesuits had been expelled from France as early as 1764. But it was only by the Law of February 13, 1790, that the Revolution declared that monastic vows were no longer recognized in France, and that orders and congregations in which such vows were made were forever suppressed. By this decree congregations of simple vows were not 'legally' affected. But the eleventh of the Organic Articles of 1802 implicitly prohibited even congregations; declaring that all ecclesiastical establishments except chapters and seminaries were suppressed. Two years later, however, 'authorized' congregations were allowed. But only such had legal standing.[123]

These attacks upon religious institutes continued into the nineteenth century. In 1855 Pope Pius IX protested against the efforts of Cavour to suppress religious institutes in Sardinia. In his allocution "*Probe memineritis*,"[124] he protests against the

[120] Const. "*Alias ad apostolatus*," 30 Jan. 1768—*Fontes*, n. 464.

[121] Clement XIV, litt. ap., "*Dominus ac Redemptor*," July 21, 1773—Parsons, *Studies in Church History*, IV, 487; Prestage, "Pombal," *Cath. Encycl.*, XII, 224.

[122] "Choiseul," *Cath. Encycl.*, III, 695.

[123] Goyau, "France," *Cath. Encycl.*, VI, 166.

[124] 22 January 1855—*Fontes*, n. 519.

laws which proposed to abolish monasteries and religious institutes in order that the government might seize their property. In another document of the same year he declared that these laws were null and void and that those who had proposed and favored them had incurred the ecclesiastical penalties.[125]

The philosophy of oppression even found its way to America. In 1851 the Jesuits were expelled from Colombia in South America, and ten years later laws were passed that were most severe and unjust. Not only were churches and religious institutes despoiled, but even hospitals and asylums. The Church was denied the right to acquire or possess property. What individual churches had was robbed from them and the churches turned into barracks. Nuns were driven from their convents without any provision being made for their support. Religious institutes were civilly interdicted; and those who refused to obey these laws were sent into exile or prison.[126]

Against these laws in particular Pope Pius IX protested on three different occasions: By the allocutions "*Acerbissimum*" of 22 September 1852,[127] and "*Meminit unusquisque,*" of 20 September 1861,[128] and especially by the encyclical "*Incredibili,*" of September 17, 1863.[129] But in the following year this same Pope issued the famous encyclical "*Quanta cura,*" in which he exposed the false philosophy of government underlying the attacks on the Church and religious institutes. Declaring that the divine origin of the Church had been denied in order to destroy its power over men and nations, the Pope states that the theory was then introduced that the best form of government was one which refused any recognition whatever to religion and allowed to all the right to preach and publish any doctrine, even the most outrageous, in the name of liberty of conscience. But under such

---

125 Allocut. "*Cum saepe,*" 26 July 1855—*Fontes*, n. 520.

126 Cf. Pius IX, ep. encyl: "*Incredibile,*" 17 Sept. 1863—*Fontes*, n. 537.

127 *Fontes*, n. 515.

128 *Acta Pii IX*, III, 281-287.

129 *Fontes*, n. 537.

a system, he points out that religion and justice ceased to be the props of government and the only law was force and the blind will of the people. With higher motives removed, there remained only the motives of greed, ambition, and cupidity. Then under the lead of the enemies of religion it was inevitable that the Church and religious institutes should become the first victims. The Pope after this reprobated the pernicious influence of Socialism and Communism and condemned each of the false doctrines. Pertinent to this outline are the following condemned propositions:

> 26.—The Church has not an innate and legitimate right to acquire and possess property;
> 30.—The immunity of the Church and of ecclesiastical persons has its origin in the civil law;
> 53.—Laws which protect the status of religious institutes and deal with their rights and duties, should be abrogated . . . and the civil government can entirely suppress religious institutes . . . and subject and hand over to the administration and will of the civil power, their goods and revenues.[130]

These and many other false doctrines were condemned by the Pope in the above mentioned 'Syllabus.' Though this action undoubtedly had widespread effect, it cannot be said that an era of complete tranquillity set in for religion. In France under the Third Republic (1875) and the influence of the Masonic Lodges a wave of anti-clericalism surged up against the Church and religious institutes. The Jesuits were again dissolved and other congregations could exist only when authorized. The attack was renewed again at the turn of the Century when by ten articles of the Laws of 1901, religious institutes existing without a charter were dissolved and their members expatriated. In the next few years in France the laws were made still more drastic. By the infamous laws of Association of 1905, an effort was made to overthrow the Church and to substitute 'associations of wor-

[130] Pius IX, ep. encyl. *"Quanta cura,"* 8 Dec. 1864—*Fontes*, n. 542; *Syllabus errorum,—Fontes*, n. 543.

ship,' giving to the laity the right to appoint the bishop and pastor and to remove them at will. Typical of the *sang froid* with which the Church was robbed is the following:

> To the Clergyman doing duty at Azay-sur-Indre.
>
> SIR:
>
> In execution of the law of 1881, and in default of any Catholic worship declaration, I have the honor to inform you that the Commune today takes possession of the presbytery and Church, which you are invited to quit immediately. In case of your refusal to do so, a contravention summons, according to the law, will be prepared against you. Please, sir, accept the assurance of my consideration.
>
> THE MAYOR,
> *Boucher.*
>
> Azay-sur-Indre,
> 16 Dec. 1906.[181]

The Code in canon 531 vindicates once again the right of the institute, province and house to acquire and possess property. But the mere mention of Russia, Germany, Spain and Mexico—and these are only the worst offenders—will indicate that civilly there is still *something* to be desired.

ARTICLE III. COMMENTARY

CANON 531

"Non modo religio, sed etiam provincia et domus sunt capaces acquirendi et possidendi bona temporalia cum reditibus stabilibus seu fundatis, nisi earum capacitas in regulis et constitutionibus excludatur aut coarctetur."

Canon 531 states those units of religious institutes which are endowed by common law with capacity to acquire and possess property and the circumstances under which this capacity is restricted or excluded.

---

[181] Cf. J. F. Boyd, "The Ecclesiastical Revolution in France," *AER*, XXXVI (1907), 125.

The meaning and the division of property and the meaning of acquisition and possession have already been considered in Part I of this chapter. This Part will treat of the nature and origin of the canonical right to own property; of the restrictions on this right; of the subject and object of this right; and of the penalties for violating this right.

1. NATURE AND ORIGIN OF THE CANONICAL RIGHT TO OWN PROPERTY.

The right to own property is in general derived from natural law. As Pope Leo XIII has said: "Man has received from nature the right to the private possession of property."[132] The right to form associations for legitimate purposes is also a natural right.[133] Consequently honest associations of individuals have a natural right to own property.

Now, though it is true that the property right of religious societies is not well understood until consideration be given to the canonical personality bestowed on these societies by ecclesiastical authority, still it is proper to emphasize somewhat the natural right enjoyed by the associated members—a right which is neither renounced by the vows[134] nor destroyed by the grant of moral personality. In the past religious institutes have been despoiled of their property by civil governments on the pretext that no injury was being done to the members, since the property belonged not to the members but to the moral person created by the Church.[135] This flimsy pretext not only denies to the Church the right to create moral persons, but to honest associations the natural right to own property. Perhaps it is for

---

[132] "Possidere res privatim ut suas, jus est homini a natura data."—Leo XIII, litt. encycl. *"Rerum Novarum,"* May 15, 1891, n. 4—*Fontes*, n. 611.

[133] "Il dirrito di associarsi con altri, per fine onesto, viene dalla natura, non dalla legge: per la ragione che, quando il fine è onesto, l'uomo è libero di adoperare tutti i mezzi che sono leciti, per conseguirlo . . ."—Liberatore, *Chiesa e Stato*, p. 228.

[134] Augustine, *A Commentary*, III, 175.

[135] Vermeersch, *De Religiosis*, II (91).

the sake of emphasizing this right that the Sacred Congregation of Religious, especially since the concordat with Italy, has inserted in some constitutions the text of canon 531, but omitting from it the clause *"nisi earum capacitas in regulis et constitutionibus excludatur aut coarctetur."*[136]

The natural right of the Catholic Church and of the Holy See to the free and independent ownership of property is vindicated by the Code in canon 1495 § 1. Without giving further consideration to this natural right, the Code in § 2 of this same canon claims the right of the ecclesiastical authority to bestow the canonical right to the ownership of property on moral persons created or established by this same authority. The origin, then, of the patrimonial right of the religious institute, province, and house, is the moral personality bestowed on them by ecclesiastical authority. The elements which constituted the former religious group or association undergo no material change. Nevertheless, the ecclesiastical authority builds upon these elements a new juridical entity. This entity, in as far as it can be distinguished from the elements which compose it, and not the members, is the new subject of rights and duties.[137] Among these rights is that with which this study is concerned, viz., the right to own property. The property, then, of the religious corporation is not the property of the members. It is the property of the moral person or ecclesiastical corporation.[138]

How is moral personality acquired?

Moral personality comes to a religious *society* either by prescript of law, or by a special grant made by a competent ec-

---

[136] Larraona, "Commentarium Codicis," *CpR,* XII (1931), 252.

[137] The members, however, continue to play an essential part in the exercise of these rights and duties.—There are many theories about the exact nature of the 'moral person.' They are discussed by Vermeersch, "De Persona Morali," *Periodica,* XXIV (1935), pp. 1*-17*. On page 13* he says: "Verae tamen sunt relationes ad finem communem, vera iura et officia quibus tenentur socii. Socii cum istis relationibus sunt verae personae morales." This view is important because of the possibility of confiscation mentioned above.

[138] Canon 1499 § 2.

clesiastical superior through a formal decree.[139] No difficulty is experienced where a formal decree of erection has been issued to a religious society, as the decree is proof of personality and the consequent patrimonial right; though, as is clear, the constitutions may restrict or prohibit the exercise of this right. By a decree of the Sacred Congregation of Religious in 1922, all bishops were to inquire into the canonical erection of all religious congregations within their territory. If any were found lacking a formal decree of erection, a formal decree was to be issued declaring them canonically erected as diocesan institutes. This decree was to have the effect of curing the want of canonical erection, as far as need be, for the past.[140]

The Code itself makes provision for *provinces* of religious institutes of pontifical right since it states that only the Holy See may establish them.[141] In regard to these the moral personality and therefore the origin of the right to property is clear.

In order to erect religious *houses* into ecclesiastical moral persons, no formal decree to that effect is necesary.[142] Such houses are moral persons by prescript of law. But where moral personality has been conferred by prescript of law, it is, as Vromant points out, oftentimes only in passing and as it were accidentally that the Code indicates the various subjects of this personality.[143] Fortunately, however, the Code indicates clearly that the religious house is a moral person by stating in canon 531, that not only the institute but also the province and the house have the right to acquire and possess temporal goods unless this right is restricted or excluded in their rules and constitutions. Even when the right to own property is not restricted by the rules and constitutions, it is not an absolute right, but one granted *"ad normam sacrorum canonum."*[144] In virtue

[139] Canon 100 § 1.

[140] Decretum, Nov. 30, 1932, n. II—*AAS,* XIV (1922), 644.

[141] Canon 494 § 1.

[142] Cf. canon 497 § 1.

[143] *De Bonis Eccl. Temp.,* n. 15.

[144] Canon 1495 § 2.

of this prescript the moral person obliges itself to follow out all regulations and prescriptions—even to submit to the restriction or suppression of its right—if the ecclesiastical authority considers this necessary. Some of these canonical regulations of the right of property are:

1. Religious societies of pontifical right that are not mendicants are forbidden to acquire property by begging without the special permission of the Holy See.[145]

2. This same prohibition is binding on diocesan institutes unless they have the permission of their local ordinary and comply with the other prescriptions of canon 622 § 3.[146]

3. Regulars who are also mendicants may beg alms in their own diocese with no permission but that of their superiors. But if they go outside their diocese they need the written permission of the ordinary of the place where they desire to beg.[147]

4. If religious societies acquire property by prescription, they must comply with the civil laws of their locality as well as the canon law on prescription.[148] But under no circumstances may they obtain by prescription what could otherwise come to them only by apostolic privilege.[149]

5. Religious cannot obtain Mass stipends by prescription; nor in that way free themselves from the obligation to say Masses.[150]

2. RESTRICTION OF THE CANONICAL RIGHT TO OWN PROPERTY.

Though all moral ecclesiastical persons have by common law the right to own property,[151] still by particular law the exercise

---

[145] Canon 622 § 1.

[146] Canon 622 §§ 2, 3.

[147] Canon 621 § 1.

[148] Canons 1508; 1510-1512.

[149] Canon 1509, 2°.

[150] Canon 1509, 5°, 8°.

[151] Canon 1495 § 2.

of this right may be prohibited in whole or in part.[152] This is especially true of religious moral persons. Among them, as Larraona states, we may find almost every possible variety of restriction.[153] Thus the Friars Minor and the Capuchins are not allowed even the common ownership of property.[154] Whatever the individual or the order acquires is acquired for the Holy See.[155] In the Society of Jesus no capacity to acquire ownership is enjoyed by the *domus professionis*.[156] Among the Discalced Carmelites houses which are not destined for missions are allowed to have their own income only in special cases.[157] In the Claretian Congregation capacity is not limited, but that of the province and house is subordinate. In other congregations only the institute as such may own property.[158]

From these examples—only a few of many possible ones—it can be seen that the restriction of the right to own property may affect the right itself, so as to exclude it or limit it; or it may qualify the right, so as to determine the kind of property that may be possessed, or the manner in which it may be possessed. These restrictions are not imposed or proposed by the common law of the Church. Yet they are not contrary to the common law. Provision is made for these restrictions by the text of canon 531 which states that the institute, province, and house have capacity to own property unless this capacity is limited or excluded by their rules and constitutions. Under the heading of "rules and constitutions" are likewise included those statutes of the institute, whether provincial or general, which have the force of law, and also prescripts of the Holy See.[159] But restrictions

[152] ". . . nisi earum capacitas in regulis et constitutionibus excludatur aut coarctetur."—Canon 531.

[153] "Commentarium Codicis," *CpR*, XII (1931), 251.

[154] C. of Trent, Sess. XXV, *de regularibus*, c. 3.

[155] Canon 582 § 2.

[156] Oswald, *Commentarium in decem partes constitutionum S. J.*, nn. 691-725.

[157] *Constitutions O.C.D.*, nn. 617, 631.

[158] Vromant, *De Bonis Eccl. Temp.*, n. 229.

[159] Larraona, "Commentarium Codicis," *CpR*, XII (1931), 252.

must be clearly stated, and their validity be unquestioned. The capacity by common law is clear and certain and can be denied or limited only by a clear and certain particular law. If the rules and constitutions are silent the capacity cannot be questioned.

3. SUBJECT OF THE RIGHT TO OWN PROPERTY.

General Remarks.—The subject in whom vests the ownership of ecclesiastical property is, according to canon 1499 §. 2, the moral person that has legitimately acquired it.[160] This law applies also to the ownership of religious ecclesiastical property. Canon 531 in stating that the religious institute, province, and house have capacity to acquire temporal goods, mentions the usual owners of religious ecclesiastical property, but not the only possible ones. As will be seen, there are other possible proprietors of religious property.

In the first place mention may be made of the supreme authority over all ecclesiastical property, even religious, which is vested in the Sovereign Pontiff. Though it is true that this is not ownership in the strict sense,[161] still papal law is the norm for the possession and administration of all ecclesiastical property.[162] Moreover, if the need or utility of the Church require it, the Pope can limit, even transfer the ownership of ecclesiastical property no matter what moral person has title to it.[163] This, according to Vromant, is an implicit obligation accepted by all ecclesiastical corporations.[164]

---

[160] "Dominium bonorum, sub suprema auctoritate Sedis Apostolicae, ad eam pertinet moralem personam, quae eadem bona legitime acquisiverit."

[161] *Summa*, II-II, q. 100, art. 1, ad 7.

[162] Canons 1495 § 2; 1499 § 2; 1518 cf. Pistocchi, *De Bonis Eccl. Temp.*, pp. 69-71.

[163] "Supremam auctoritatem in bona ecclesiastica Sedes Apostolica exercet. Quae auctoritas ad meram vigilantiam in administrationem rerum restringi nequit, sed eo usque se extendit, quo suprema potestas jurisdictionis Romano Pontifici propria est (Can. 218 § 1)."—Pejska, *Jus Canonicum Religiosorum*, p. 60.

[164] *De Bonis Eccl. Temp.*, n. 48; cf. also Pruemmer, *Manuale J. C.*, q. 443.

In a more exact sense the Holy See acquires ownership of the property of those religious societies which by their rules and constitutions are forbidden to own temporal goods. This is clear from canon 582,2°, which states that if the order is incapable of acquiring property, all property that comes to members solemnly professed is acquired for the Holy See as proprietor. The proprietorship of the Holy See is also clear from a response mentioned by Fanfani. To the question whether it was allowed to renounce an inheritance left either to a regular, or to an institute lacking capacity to acquire property, the answer was: In the negative, without consulting the Holy See, since to do so would injure the *ius ad rem* already acquired by the Holy See.[165]

Another possible subject of the ownership of religious property would be a moral person existing within a religious institute in virtue of particular law, or legitimately erected by a competent religious superior. The institute, the province, and the house, as is clear, are subjects of the patrimonial right by common law. However there would be no obstacle to the erection of other moral persons by prescript of particular law; nor would a religious ordinary exceed his power by creating a moral person through his formal decree. Thus, where several religious provinces of the same institute exist within the jurisdiction of a single civil government, a superior general might establish a vicariate over that territory. Likewise several provinces could conduct jointly a house of higher studies, a publication, etc., and distinct personality might be necessary for such undertakings. In such cases the newly established moral person would have, at least by common law, capacity to acquire property, because the general law of canon 1495 § 2 is applicable.[166] However since the erection of a moral person is an act of public authority, only those religious superiors are competent who possess jurisdiction *in foro externo,* e. g., the major superiors in exempt clerical institutes.[167]

---

[165] *De Jure Religiosorum,* p. 169.

[166] Larraona, "Commentarium Codicis," *CpR,* XII (1931), 250.

[167] Canons 198; 501; Brown, *The Canonical Juristic Personality,* p. 92.

Finally there is the possibility, if papal dispensation has been obtained, of having the ownership of immovable community property vested in one or more of the religious, even though these religious have pronounced the solemn vow of poverty. Permission to acquire, retain, and administer their common property was first granted to regulars of Belgium and Holland by a rescript of the Sacred Penitentiary in 1820. This rescript was confirmed again in 1878. The purpose of it was to protect the property of the religious from confiscation by civil governments.[168] In the opinion of Bouix, this indult merely allowed the religious to act as civil owners without giving them any real ownership.[169] But arguing from the fact that renewal of the indult was asked on the grounds that the community property would be confiscated unless *real* ownership was vested in the religious, Vermeersch holds that the indult of 1878 was intended to grant full protection to the religious against the civil laws, and therefore allowed the individual religious, when necessary, to have *real* ownership of the community property.[170]

In India ecclesiastical property, by permission of the Sacred Congregation for the Propagation of the Faith, was retained either by the Christian communities in their own name, or by ecclesiastical superiors as private possessors.[171] Since the purpose of this permission was to protect the property of the Church religious could avail themselves of it as well as seculars.

However, in all cases where the Church property was owned by others the administration of it was reserved to ecclesiastical superiors.

These preliminary remarks pave the way for a consideration of the subjects by common law of the ownership of religious ecclesiastical property. As indicated in canon 531, they are the institute, the province, and the house.

---

[168] Leo XIII, indultum, 31 July 1878—Vermeersch, *De Rel.*, II, (81).

[169] *De Jure Regularium,* I, 350.

[170] *De Religiosis,* II, (87).

[171] S.C.P.F., litt. encycl., *Vicariis Apostolicis Indiarum Orientalium—Coll. Lacensis,* VI, col. 667.

In this part of the commentary it will be presumed that the subject has capacity to acquire and possess property. For restrictions on this capacity the reader is referred to what has been said on pp. 37, 38, of this chapter.

The Religious Institute.—By a religious institute or '*religio*' is meant every society, approved by legitimate ecclesiastical authority, whose members strive after evangelical perfection by observing the special laws of their society, and by pronouncing the public vows of religion. This is the canonical definition of a religious institute as found in canon 488, 1°, and therefore the meaning of *religio* as used in canon 531. In this study no special mention is made of those who live in communities but do not take public vows. It may be here noted, however, that their institutes, provinces and houses are moral persons with capacity to acquire property. The administration of this property is regulated by the same laws that are stated in this work.

Religio is sometimes used in a collective sense to indicate, for example, all Franciscans, all Benedictines. In this sense the Benedictines comprise not one but many different religious institutes. Each different institute has the right to own property, but the collective *religio* has not unless this right be granted by particular law.[172] The words '*ordo*' and '*congregatio religiosa*,' as used in the Code, have the same meaning as *religio* for the purpose of canon 531. *Religio* is the generic term, of which *ordo* and *congregatio religiosa* are species.[173]

Every religious institute has by common law the right to acquire and retain the ownership of temporal goods, unless its rules or constitutions limit or exclude this right. However, as already stated, such limitation or exclusion must be clearly expressed. Silence is to be interpreted in favor of the right, since the right is in possession in virtue of canon 531.

---

[172] Larraona, "Commentarium Codicis," *CpR*, XII (1931), 247.

[173] Cf. canon 488,2°; Schaefer, *De Religiosis*, p. 36. It is beyond the scope of this study to go into more details about the meaning of religio. A fuller explanation may be found in standard authors.

The *manner* in which property may be acquired is in general every way that is allowed by natural or positive law and not excluded by canon law.[174] The usual way that the institute has of acquiring property is by a tax on the provinces, by legacies and donations, by investments.

The *amount* of property that may be acquired is not determined by canon law.

As to the *duration* of this right, the right endures until the religious institute is suppressed or becomes extinct.[175] The Holy See is the only authority that can suppress a religious institute, even though it be diocesan and consist of but a single house. In all cases of suppression of an institute it belongs to the Holy See alone to determine about the property of the suppressed institute, safeguarding, however, the intention of the donors.[176]

In the matter of suppression of a religious institute, it is evident that the general law of canon 1501 has been supplemented by canon 493; otherwise the property of a suppressed diocesan institute would belong to the diocese in which the institute was located, and would not be at the disposal of the Holy See.

What has been said of suppressed institutes is applicable by analogy of law to institutes that have become extinct for lack of members or for other causes.[177]

By analogy with canon 494 § 1, it would seem that the suppression of a monastic congregation is a matter that belongs to the Holy See. In the event of suppression, that authority would determine about the property. However, if the individual mon-

---

[174] Canon 1499 § 1; cf. above, pp. 37-38.

[175] *Per se* a moral person is perpetual, and by a fiction of law even endures for a hundred years after it has ceased to exist.—Canon 102 § 1.

[176] Canon 493: Permission to suppress a religious institute is obtained from the Sacred Congregation of Religious, or from the Sacred Congregation for the Propagation of the Faith if the institute is subject to this Congregation.

[177] Larraona, "Commentarium Codicis," *CpR*, XII (1931), 247.

asteries were not suppressed along with the congregation, it is probable that the property would be divided among them.[178]

THE PROVINCE.—The second subject of the ownership of religious ecclesiastical property mentioned in canon 531 is the province.

A religious province according to canon 488, 6°, is the union under the same superior of several houses that form part of the same religious institute.[179] As will be seen later, each house, unless forbidden by the constitutions, has the right to the ownership of property. By their incorporation into a province the right of each house is neither lost nor blended into a single or collective right, but a new moral person possessed of a distinct right to own property is created.

The province has its own superior and its own officials and administration. Its existence dates from the moment when the rescript of erection is executed.[180] Once legitimately erected the province is a juridical person with capacity to own property.

As to the *manner* of acquiring property, the province, like the institute, may acquire property in every way that is allowed by natural or positive law and not excluded by canon law. The usual way for it to acquire property is by a tax on the houses, by donations, legacies, and investments.

The *amount* of property which a province may acquire is not limited by common law. If there is to be a limitation it must be determined by the particular law of the institute. Usually the constitutions provide for the support of the *Curia Generalitia* by a tax on the provinces, and in some cases give the supreme moderator the faculty to impose an additional tax to meet extraordinary emergencies.[181] As an index of what can be done in this regard, article 294 of the *Normae* of 1901 proposes that at

---

[178] Fanfani, *De Jure Religiosorum*, p. 27.

[179] "Provinciae [nomine] plurium religiosarum domorum inter se coniunctio sub eodem Superiore, partem eiusdem religionis constituens."

[180] Larraona, "Commentarium Codicis," *CpR*, XII (1931), 248.

[181] Vromant, *De Bonis Eccl. Temp.*, n. 35 bis.

the end of each year each province should send a third of its net income to the general treasury.[182] Some recent constitutions follow this norm,[183] and the instruction of the Sacred Congregation of Religious of March 25, 1922 indicates that it should be followed.[184]

Over and above what is expressly stated in the constitutions, it seems that the supreme moderator of centralized institutes can, without violation of the constitutions, oblige inferior officials to make reasonable donations from their treasuries to the general treasury, whenever the scope of the institute makes this necessary. To deny this would result in having the work of the institute impeded, or at least retarded by a branch of the institute. However, in no case may a general superior suppress the administration in a province so as to have the general administration administer the property of the province. Neither may the general superior arbitrarily despoil a province of its property or any part thereof.[185]

If a province is *circumscribed* by the addition of, or withdrawal of one or more houses, it may be necessary, unless otherwise provided for by the constitutions, for the general chapter or the supreme moderator with his consultors to make a readjustment of provincial property in order to compensate any losses occasioned by the change. But the houses affected in the change retain the property that they had, for the reason that this property belongs to the house and not to the province.[186]

The *division* of a province of pontifical right for the purpose of forming two or more religious provinces from the territory that formerly belonged to a single province, can only be effected

[182] *Normae secundum quas S. Cong. EP. et Reg. procedere solet in approbandis novis institutis votorum simplicium,* Romae, June 28, 1901.

[183] Vromant, *De Bonis Eccl. Temp.*, n. 35 bis.

[184] Cf. nn. 62, 63—*AAS,* XV (1923), 459.

[185] Vermeersch-Creusen, *Epitome,* I, n. 556; Pejska, *Jus Canonicum Religiosorum,* p. 61.

[186] Pejska, *Jus Canonicum Religiosorum,* p. 62.

by the Holy See.[187] The division of the property, by analogy, should proceed according to the norm of canon 1500, i. e., the property, and likewise the debts, should be divided so that each of the provinces formed from the old territory shall have an equitable share. In making this division care must be taken to safeguard the intention of the donors, acquired rights of others, and particular law.[188] The authority competent to make this division of property, unless the constitutions state otherwise, is the general chapter or, if it is not in session, the supreme moderator with his consultors.[189]

In regard to the *suppression* of a religious province, it should again be noted that if the province is of pontifical right, this can be done only by the Holy See. If the province is of diocesan right and all the houses are in the same diocese, the local ordinary, saving the particular law of the institute, can suppress the province. If the houses are in several dioceses, all the ordinaries concerned must concur.

The property of a suppressed pontifical province is at the disposal of the general chapter of the institute, or if the chapter is not in session, of the supreme moderator with his or her consultors.[190] The same rule would seem to be applicable to provinces of diocesan institutes.[191] But as already stated, the intention of the donors and the laws of justice must be safeguarded.

The canon does not state whether the vote of the consultors should be deliberative or merely consultative. Augustine and Cocchi say it should be deliberative.[192] Vermeersch and Schaefer

---

187 Canon 494 § 1.

188 Canon 1500.

189 Larraona, "Commentarium Codicis," *CpR,* XII (1931), 249; cf. also canon 494 § 2.

190 Canon 494 § 2.

191 Cf. Schaefer, *De Religiosis,* p. 88.

192 Augustine, *A Commentary,* III, 80; Cocchi, *Commentarium,* III, 31.

say that a merely consultative vote is not excluded.[193] It would be difficult to prove that this latter view is incorrect.

The procedure of the general chapter or superior general in disposing of such property is not accurately determined. According to Augustine, in the bulls of suppression of various orders a formula occurs which seems to indicate the "laws of justice" and the "will of the founders." Liabilities of the suppressed province must be assumed; the divine worship may not be curtailed; the obligations towards charitable purposes must be fulfilled; and in particular must the Mass obligations be strictly complied with. Eventual pensions or apportionments must be defrayed from the revenues of the suppressed province, and the rest may be employed for the purposes of the whole institute.[194]

THE VICE-PROVINCE.—Many religious institutes have extended their apostolic labors into mission fields far distant from their general and provincial houses. For the better government of these missions it is often necessary to appoint a special superior and grant the territory a certain amount of independence of the province with which it is connected. When subject to a religious province the name given to this territory is usually that of 'vice-province' or 'quasi-province,' and the superior is known as the vice-provincial.[195] There is no legislation in the Code concerning the vice-province. Its government must depend on the constitutions of the institute with which it is connected. If these are silent it would seem that the superior general of exempt clerical institutes with his consultors has the faculty to establish a vice-province and appoint its superior.[196] Whether or not the vice-province has capacity to own property will depend on

---

[193] Vermeersch-Creusen, *Epit.*, I, n. 556; Schaefer, *De Rel.*, p. 88, not. 5.

[194] Augustine, *A Commentary*, III, 80.

[195] No consideration is given here to those vice-provinces which in certain institutes are completely independent and erected by the Holy See. In common law they are equal to provinces. Cf. Larraona, "Commentarium Codicis," *CpR*, XII (1931), 248.

[196] Cf. above, p. 40.

the decree of erection. If it lacks this capacity, it may still have a certain amount of administrative autonomy, but the property will belong to the province.[197] If capacity to own property has been granted the vice-province, it must for practical purposes be subject to the laws governing provincial property except that in the event of suppression the property would revert to the province according to canon 1501 and not be at the disposal of the supreme moderator or of the general chapter.[198]

THE HOUSE.—The third subject of ownership of religious ecclesiastical property according to the common law of the Church is the religious house.

In a general way any house or residence that belongs to a religious institute may be called a religious house. Specifically, in the sense of canon 531, by a religious house is meant a permanent (*stabilis*) and canonically established foundation where religious of the same institute practice the common life according to their constitutions and subject to their own superior. If a building in which religious dwell has no regularly assigned community, or has not been canonically erected as a religious house, it does not come within the scope of canon 531. This is usually the case with what are known as affiliated houses, farms, summer homes, villas; also schools, hospitals, orphanages and other ecclesiastical institutions.[199] However, this is a general statement referring not to the facts but to the common law. To determine exactly the status of such places, it is necessary to consult the particular law of each institute.

The *time* when a house has the right to acquire and possess property is the moment when it is canonically erected. However, apart from the particular law of the institute, there is no norm by which the time of the canonical erection of a house may

---

197 Larraona, "Commentarium Codicis," *CpR*, XII (1931), 248, note 454.

198 Pejska, *Jus Canonicum, C.Ss.R.*, p. 91.

199 Pejska, *Jus Canonicum Religiosorum*, p. 49. Charitable and religious institutions can, of course, be moral persons and own property, but are rather known as 'ecclesiastical institutions' than as religious houses, though the latter term was once common. Cf. canons 1489-1494.

be determined. Common law does not demand any formal decree of erection in the case of religious houses.[200] When the proper ecclesiastical authority has given permission and when the will of the religious superior to erect a house has been externally manifested, the house is erected *ex ipso praescripto iuris,* and is a moral person with capacity to acquire and possess property. In regard, however, to the erection of houses, strictly so called, too much importance cannot be placed on the need of getting the permission of the proper ecclesiastical authority. Lacking this permission the house would not be legitimately established and eventually a rectification of the defect would be required in order to confer upon the house a true, canonical status.[201]

The house like the province and institute may acquire property in every way that is allowed by natural or positive law and not excluded by canon law or by the particular law of the institute. The usual way it has of acquiring property is by donations, legacies and the industry of the members. Canon 580 § 2 states that whatever the religious acquires by his industry or because of his religious character, he acquires for his institute.[202] By institute is meant either the house, or the province, or the general curia, as is evident from canon 594 § 2. The particular law of the institute will decide which moral person acquires possession in such cases.

That a minimum *amount,* or at least a well founded hope of property is necessary for all houses to be erected is evident from canon 496, where it is stated that no house should be erected unless it is prudently judged that decent support and lodging will be provided for the members from the revenues of the foundation or from the customary alms or in some other way. No maximum amount is determined by the common law of the Church. The constitutions of the institute decide in regard to

---

[200] Larraona, "Commentarium Codicis," *CpR,* XII (1931), 249.

[201] Pejska, *Jus Canonicum Religiosorum,* p. 55; cf. also, S.C.P.F., litt., 7 dec. 1901—*ASS,* XXXIV (1898), 639.

[202] Cf. also canon 582.

this. However, as it is usual to tax the province for the support of the general curia, so it is customary to tax the houses for the support of the provincial curia and to carry out works undertaken by the province. Here again the *Normae* of 1901 may be used as a guide, especially article 294, which suggests that each house at the end of the year should contribute one-third of its net income to the provincial treasury.[203]

Since the *separation* of a house from one province in order to unite it to another changes the limits of these provinces, the faculty to do this rests only with the Holy See, if the institute is of ponifical right.[204] In such a case, though the common property of the province should be divided *ex bono et aequo,* the property of the house or houses concerned remains at it was before the change and the ownership of the house is left undisturbed.[205]

The *suppression* of a religious house seldom takes place without the need of making some disposition of its property. As already stated, if a diocesan house is to be suppressed, so that the institute is suppressed with it, then only the Holy See can do this; and to it is also reserved the right to determine about the property.[206] If it is one of several houses belonging to a diocesan institute, the ordinary of the diocese in which it is located has authority to suppress it. But he must hear the opinion of the highest superior of the institute and recourse to the Holy See with suspensive effect is allowed against his decree.[207] The property of the suppressed house becomes the property of the province, or of the institute if there is no province.[208]

If the house to be suppressed belongs to a pontifical institute, the *beneplacitum* of the Holy See is required if it is an

---

[203] *Normae secundum quas S.C.Ep. et Reg. procedere solet in approbandis novis institutis votorum simplicium,* Romae, 28 June 1901.

[204] Canon 494 § 1.

[205] Pejska, *Jus Canonicum Religiosorum,* pp. 57, 62.

[206] Canon 493.

[207] Canon 498.

[208] Canon 1501.

exempt institute; otherwise the supreme moderator has the power, provided the local ordinary consents to the suppression.[209] In either case the property of the house becomes the property of the next higher moral person in the institute.[210] However, the property of all suppressed houses is at all times subject to the conditions stated in canon 1501, i. e., the will of the donors, acquired rights, and particular laws must always be safeguarded before any disposition is made of the property. So also, permission of the proper authority, according to the norm of canon 1532, is necessary if the suppression is accompanied by alienation of property.[211] However, the transfer of property to the next higher moral person of the institute is not considered as alienation.

4. OBJECT OF THE CANONICAL RIGHT TO OWN PROPERTY.

The kind of property which a religious moral person may acquire is stated in the Code by the general term *bona temporalia.* It has already been indicated[212] that the manner of acquiring property is subject to various regulations. But the kind of property that may be acquired is not limited by the Code. These two should not be confused. The insertion of the clause "*cum reditibus stabilibus seu fundatis*" in the text of canon 531 was not made to exclude other kinds of property, nor was it necessary after using the general term *bona temporalia.* But it was inserted, according to Larraona, for historical and juridical reasons.[213] The sense of the word '*seu*' may be disjunctive or conjunctive.[214] But in either case the nature of the income would be the same, i. e., a permanent or steady income, such as

209 Canon 498.

210 Canon 1501.

211 Schaefer, *De Religiosis,* n. 88; Pruemmer, *Manuale, J. C.,* q. 182.

212 Above, pp. 37, 38.

213 "Commentarium Codicis," *CpR,* XII (1931), 250.

214 Oesterle, *Praelectiones J. C.,* I, 276.

that from bonds, bank deposits, rentals, investments, and endowments; and in contradistinction to income of an unsteady character, such as free-will offerings.[215]

5. PENALTIES FOR VIOLATION OF THE CANONICAL RIGHT TO PROPERTY.

The right of ecclesiastical moral persons to the property they have legitimately acquired is protected against those who would dare to usurp it or hinder its use by an excommunication that is simply reserved to the Holy See.[216]

To incur this penalty, it is necessary that the act be presumptuous—"*si quis . . . praesumpserit.*"[217] Hence, fear of any kind, ignorance of any kind, except affected ignorance, and all circumstances that diminish the imputability of the act, excuse from the penalty. Secondly, the amount of property concerned must be such that in the matter of theft it would constitute grave matter. If this is the case, and there is no excuse for the act the penalty is incurred whenever ecclesiastical property is usurped or converted to one's own use, or when the fruits of it are prevented from reaching the ones to whom they are rightfully due.

These headings embrace almost every form of injury that can be done to the right to own property. Under usurpation is included every act by which ecclesiastical property is taken, under some pretext of right, with the intention of making it one's

---

[215] For information on the specific ways of acquiring property the reader is referred to the various books on that subject, especially to a dissertation by the Rev. W. J. Doheny, C.S.C., on *Church Property: Modes of Acquisition,* Catholic University of America, Canon Law Studies n. 41, Washington, D. C., 1927. Here it may be mentioned that the principal means of acquiring religious ecclesiastical property are by pious foundations, by inheritance and legacies, by alms and prescription.

[216] Canon 2346. Cf. Raus, *Institutiones Canonicae,* n. 467.

[217] It is not necessary to act personally. One who acts through a procurator or agent or otherwise, as mentioned in canon 2209, is excommunicated.

own.[218] It is of no importance what kind of property is taken,[219] or whether the usurpation is on the strength of public or private authority. Neither is one excused from the penalty on the grounds that the action is civilly valid.[220]

To convert to one's own use could include not only those who usurp, but also those who after usurpation receive or buy church property and turn it to their own use. In the opinion of Cappello, the legality of the transaction by which the property is acquired in no way excuses from the penalty, provided it is known that the property belongs to the Church.[221] Those who rent usurped property are excommunicated,[222] but those who alienate church property are not included under the penalty of this canon.[223]

Not only the property itself, but the fruit or revenues of the property are protected by this canon. Thus, those who prevent the revenues of ecclesiastical property from accruing to the rightful owners fall under the same excommunication as those who usurp or convert the property to their own use. A decree similar to this canon had been issued by the Council of Trent.[224] Because it used the wording "*usurpare SEU impedire,*" authors considered the two verbs as coextensive in meaning. In the new legislation, however, as Vromant points out, the Code uses the words "*usurpare AUT impedire,*" thus indicating a new kind of

---

[218] A Coronata, *Institutiones J. C.*, IV, 435, 441.

[219] In this regard canon 2346 differs from the decree of C. of Trent which was concerned with property of value (*magni momenti*).—C. of Trent, Sess. XXII, *de reform.* c. 11. Cf. however, A Coronata (*op, .cit.* p. 440) who states as a probable opinion that even after the Code the sum should be a little more than that required for a mortal sin *in re de justitia.*

[220] Pruemmer, *Manuale J. C.*, p. 594, note 64.

[221] "Contraria sententia, attento textu legis et perspecta praxi S. Poenit. et S.C.C. caret quavis probabilitate."—*De Censuris,* n. 336.

[222] Hollweck, *Die Kirchliche Strafgesetze,* § 156, n. 28.

[223] Alienators of church property are penalized by canon 2347.

[224] Sess. XXII, *de reform.* c. 11.

delict.[225] In this sense then, those who by force, fraud or design, by theft, or sequestration or wilful destruction, divert the revenues of ecclesiastical property so that they cannot reach the proper owner, are subject to the penalty of excommunication which is simply reserved to the Holy See. Absolution from this cannot be obtained till the injury done to the moral person is repaired, i. e., till the property is restored or the impediment to receiving the revenues removed. In exceptional cases the Holy See may be asked to permit a composition.[226]

If it has been the patron of the moral person who has been guilty of the crimes mentioned, he is *ipso facto* deprived of the right of patronage.[227] If a cleric, in addition to the other penalties, he is (even by merely consenting to the crime), to be deprived of any benefices he may have and to be declared incapable of obtaining any benefice in future. Besides he must be suspended from the exercise of his orders for a period to be determined by his ordinary. With the exception of excommunication all these penalties for clerics are *ferendae sententiae*, and therefore require the usual admonition and sentence.[228]

---

[225] *De Bonis Ecclesiae Temporalibus*, n. 30. A Coronata, *Inst. J. C.*, IV, 440, note 8; 442, note 1; Cappello, *De Censuris*, nn. 328, 343.

[226] Composition consists in making some offer to the moral person that has been injured. If this is satisfactory under the circumstances, the Holy See allows the property to be retained. Cf. Vromant, *De Bonis Eccl. Temp.*, n. 31.

[227] Cf. canon 1448.

[228] Cf. Augustine, *A Commentary*, VIII, 392.

CHAPTER II

THE ADMINISTRATION OF PROPERTY

Article I. Historical Outline of Administration

In considering the historical development of administration attention will be paid first to what may be termed the law of the institute concerning administration, and secondly, to the law of the Church.

1. LAW OF THE INSTITUTE.

Rules and Constitutions.—Rules and constitutions are a norm of life for the religious. They state the end or purpose for which the institute has been founded and the means by which that end may be attained. Thus, the rules and constitutions, at least at present, contain norms for the administration and government of the institute as a whole, and in most cases detailed regulations regarding temporal administration. But this cannot be affirmed of all rules in the past. In the beginning rules were little more than precepts for a devout life. As stated in the last chapter of the Rule of St. Benedict: "The rules are doctrines of the holy fathers whose observance leads man to the heights of perfection."[1] As the need arose, however, prescripts were inserted into the various rules and constitutions regulating the administration of temporal goods, and recent constitutions have been required to have norms for administration before being approved.[2]

Administrators.—The first rules had few details about the administrators of temporal goods in religious institutes. Everything in this regard seems to have been left to the discretion of

[1] Regula S. Benedicti, c. 73—Logeman, *Rule of S. Benet,* p. 118.

[2] Cf. S.C. de Rel., instr., *"Inter ea,"* July 30, 1909, n. X—*Fontes,* n. 4394.

the abbot, and under him to the officials whom he appointed. In the Rule of St. Pachomius, considered as the first written rule, the *pater monasterii* is the controlling force. Nothing could be done against his will. Next in authority was the *praepositus*. His duty was similar to that of the present-day econome. At first, however, there seems to have been no obligation to appoint this official, and when appointed he was entirely subject to the abbot. Later on there was an obligation on the part of the abbot to appoint him.[3] In the Rule of St. Pachomius mention is also made of *dispensatores et ministri*. These seem to have been minor officials having the temporal goods under their care but able to dispense them only on an order from the *praepositus* or abbot.[4] Other rules mention other officials, as *decani, provisores, cellarii;* but these are only different names for similar offices or titles. Apart from imposing the obligation of having an econome, the Church in the early days did not concern itself with the titles or duties of the various administrators.

AUTHORITY OF THE ADMINISTRATORS.—There can hardly be any doubt that the Church has always desired to have ecclesiastical goods, even if belonging to religious institutes, administered by ecclesiastical persons only and not by the laity.[5] However, under the feudal system especially, lands and monasteries were sometimes accepted with only the right of use. The revenues were claimed at times by a feudal lord, at times by a lay-abbot, as, for example, when the Abbots of Aniane received a grant of exemption from Charlemagne and from Louis the Pious.[6] But the system in time became linked up with the practice of investitures and was strenuously opposed by the Church. However, even after the evil of investiture was remedied, the practice of having lay-administrators continued to a certain extent. Fer-

[3] II C. of Nice (787), c. 11—Harduin, IV, 494.

[4] Albers, "S. Pachomii . . . Regulae Monasticae"—*Florilegium Patristicum,* XVI, 36.

[5] IV C. of Carthage (398), c. 31—*MPL,* LXXXIV, 203; II C. of Nice (787), c. 11—Harduin, IV, 494.

[6] *Chartae Anianenses—MPL,* CIII, 1419.

raris states that by papal indult lay-administrators were allowed and were protected "as by a new law."[7] He shows also how under special circumstances the Holy See entered into concordats with civil governments and in these concordats concessions were made by the Holy See in regard to temporal administration. But in those cases where lay men were administrators of church property they were supposed to be under the vigilance of an ecclesiastical person.[8]

When the administration was conducted by the religious themselves the authority of the administrators had always been regulated by the rules and constitutions. The supreme authority was at first invested in the abbot; but his power was never to be used arbitrarily.[9] Even in the early rules it was forbidden to him to donate or sell anything belonging to the monastery or to do anything contrary to the prescript of the rule.[10] Later on, as already mentioned, he was obliged to have an econome. Under this plan the acts of administration were performed by the econome according to the norms of the rules and constitutions, and direction and supervision were the duty of the abbot.

Chapters.—As early as the time of St. Benedict the custom was introduced of convoking chapters or assemblies of the religious to decide on affairs of the monastery; and not infrequently these affairs had to do with temporal matters. In these meetings the abbot proposed the business in hand to the assembly and each one was allowed to give his opinion. The abbot, however, was not bound to follow these opinions, but was allowed to do what he judged best.[11] It was not till about the twelfth century that Church Law made it incumbent upon superiors to follow the decision of the chapter.[12] In the meantime, however, the chapter had undergone some evolution. Originally an as-

[7] Ferraris, "administratio," art. I, nn. 42, 43.

[8] Council of Trent, Sess. XXII, *de reform*, c. 9.

[9] C. 15, C. XVIII, q. 2.

[10] *Regula S. Aureliani, E.*, cap. 42—*MPL,* CIII, 785.

[11] Regula S. Benedicti, c. 3—Logeman, *Rule of St. Benet,* p. 17.

[12] C, I, X, *de his quae fiunt a prelato,* III, 10.

sembly of the monks of a particular monastery, it became, in the time of the Cluniac and Cistercian Congregations, an assembly of the various superiors of monasteries. In these assemblies or chapters affairs of the whole congregation were treated and sometimes a general superior was elected.[13] In 1216 Pope Innocent III, at the Fourth Lateran Council, ordered independent abbots and priors not having the custom of holding chapters to join with other abbots and priors of the same kingdom or province in celebrating chapters every three years, after the manner of the Cistercians. These chapters were to treat of reformation and regular discipline; and it is probable that under those headings some regulations were made concerning temporal administration.[14]

When the Franciscans were founded the idea of the chapter was introduced into the rule. Meetings of all the members were held every year until the members became too numerous. Later the Council of Trent obliged all monasteries to form congregations and to hold chapters.[15]

When the mendicants and religious congregations of simple vows introduced a centralized form of government into the religious life, the general chapter, composed of various superiors, became the legislative body for the institute and determined the power of all superiors in regard to temporal administration. This body, however, could not change or abrogate rules already approved by the Holy See. Under this system it became unusual, except for the purposes of election, for all the members of an institute to act in chapter, as was customary in monastic institutes. Instead of this several members were appointed or elected to act as consultors to the various superiors. The constitutions would then state when the superior needed the consent of his consultors, and when mere advice.

---

[13] Vermeersch, "Religious Life," *Cath. Encycl.*, XII, 757.

[14] IV C. of Lateran (1216), c. 12—Mansi, XXII, 999.

[15] C. of Trent, Sess. XXV, *de reg.*, cc. 1, 8; Augustine, *Commentary*, III, 107.

The constitution "*Conditae a Christo*" did not treat expressly of the chapter or of administration, except to state that the laws of each institute were to be followed.[16] However, the *Normae* of 1901,[17] and in particular the Instruction *Inter ea* of 1909, made it obligatory upon all religious institutes without exception to have general, provincial, and local consultors, and laid down special rules for their guidance.[18] These consultors have taken the place of the chapter, which is now used in most institutes only for the purpose of elections or for affairs of the institute in general.

The Code in canon 516 merely prescribes that general, provincial, and local superiors must have their consultors, and that their consent or counsel is required according to the norms of the Code and the constitutions. This is sufficient to make effective the instruction of 1909, which was prescribed for all institutes.

2. LAW OF THE CHURCH.

The earliest collections of Church Law indicate that the administration of ecclesiastical goods was in the hands of the bishop,[19] aided when necessary by minor clerics.[20] In all probability this system functioned smoothly as long as each diocese had but one parish church and one pastor who was the bishop. But when, with the growth of the Church, rural parishes became necessary; when nobles and princes began to endow churches and chapels on their estates; when the monasteries came into

---

[16] Leo XIII, const. "*Conditae a Christo,*" 8 Dec. 1900, ch. II, n. IX—*Fontes*, n. 664.

[17] *Normae secundum quas S. C. Ep. et Reg. procedere solet in approbandis novis institutis votorum simplicium,* 28 June 1901, n. 239.

[18] S.C. de Rel., instr. "*Inter ea,*" 30 July 1909, nn. 1, 5, 6, 7, 9, 13, 14—*Fontes*, n. 4394.

[19] Can. Apost. 31, 34, 37; Const. Apost. Book II, c. 25, 27, 35—Mansi, I, 323.

[20] C. of Chalcedon (451), c. 26—Harduin, II, 612; C. of Nice (787), cc 11, 12—Harduin, IV, 494.

existence with church and houses and lands; then, indeed, administration of church property became a complicated affair—so complicated that at this date it is next to impossible to say with certainty just how administration, in many cases, was conducted.

Early View of Monastic Property.—In chapter I it was seen that the first religious institutes did not owe their origin to any express design of ecclesiastical authority but were rather the result of circumstances. The first monasteries apparently were not established as ecclesiastical organizations but as more or less private undertakings to satisfy the religious needs of groups of men or women. To be sure, as Vermeersch says, they were, like all Christians, subject to the local bishop.[21] But subjection in this sense did not give the bishop control over their property any more than it did over that of the rest of the faithful. Thus, there seems to be no reason for considering the property of these monasteries as ecclesiastical goods subject to the bishop's control. This seems also to have been the view of the first founders. In writing a rule of life for the community they entrusted the administration of temporalities to themselves and to minor officials without reference to the local bishop.[22]

However, as time marched on and monasteries increased the local bishops began to take cognizance of their existence and to recognize their ecclesiastical character. The monks themselves ceased to be concerned solely with their own spiritual progress and began to engage in external activities. In this way they began to share in the alms offered by the faithful for the purposes of religion. They became beneficiaries of pious wills and testaments, and trustees of pious foundations. They received property and assistance from the bishops to aid them in establishing monasteries.[23] Under these circumstances it was clear that a portion of their property was ecclesiastical, at least from

[21] Vermeersch, *De Religiosis,* I, 30.

[22] Cf. Rules of SS. Pachomius, Basil, Benedict *et alii—MPL,* CIII *passim.*

[23] C. 73, C. XII, q. 2.

the intent of the donors. Naturally, then, the bishop, as the recognized administrator of all ecclesiastical property within his territory, would consider it his right to administer this property. But because of the peculiar nature of this property the monks were equally convinced that the right of administration belonged to them.

CONCILIAR LEGISLATION.—To what extent this conflict was waged cannot now be determined. At any rate, it became important enough to receive the attention of the Fourth General Council of Chalcedon in the year 451. This Council has often been quoted as the Council that made the monks subject to the bishop. However, this does not seem to be true to the extent that the unadorned statement would imply. Canon four of this Council takes cognizance of abuses by certain monks who, having left their convents, became mixed up both in secular and ecclesiastical affairs, and when it suited their purposes founded monasteries without leave of the bishop or any other authority. As a remedy for these abuses the Council decrees that no monastery may be built without leave of the local ordinary; and as a safeguard for monastic observance orders the monks to stay at home and "be subject to the bishop." Though the language is decisive, it is not unqualified. The prohibition which follows, about mixing in external affairs, makes it not improbable that this subjection refers to their external activities and not to their life in the monastery or to the control of temporal affairs.[24]

---

[24] "Qui vere et pure solitariam eligunt vitam, digni sunt convenienti honore. Quia tamen quidam monachi habitu utentes, res communes disturbant, indifferenter civitates circumeuntes, necnon et monasteria per se ipsos propria prasumptione constituere tentant: placuit, neminem aut aedificare aut constituere monasteria, aut oratorii domum, sine conscientia ipsius civitatis episcopi. Eos vero, qui per singulas civitates seu possessiones in monasteriis sunt, subjectos esse debere episcopo, et quieti operam dare atque observare jejunia et orationes, in locis in quibus semel Deo se devoverunt, permanentes; et neque communicare ecclesiasticis, neque saeculares aliquas tractare actiones, relinquentes propria monasteria, nisi forte jubeantur, propter urgentes necessitates, ab ipsius civitatis episcopo. Et neminem servorum suscipi in monasterium, ut sit cum eis monachus,

Canon 8 of this same Council is also important. It states that *clerics* in monasteries, etc., are subject to him who is bishop of the city. Since the emphasis is on the word *cleric,* it allows the view that not all monks in a monastery, but only those who were clerics (and therefore by reason of their ordination), were subject to the local bishop.[25] That this view is not far-fetched appears from a comparison of this text with one from the Third Council of Arles of 455, which states that the *lay* portion of a monastery is under the care of the abbot, and the bishop has nothing to do with monks that are not clerics. The reason given for this is that it is according to religion and reason that clerics be subject to the orders of the bishop; but that the lay portion of a monastery be subject only to the orders of their abbot.[26]

The last canon which shall be quoted from the Council of Chalcedon shows that in spite of the restrictions placed on the monks, the Council recognizes the right of the monks to possess property and logically, it would seem, to administer it. Canon 24 says that once a monastery has been dedicated with permission of the bishop, it remains a monastery forever after "and the things which belong to it are reserved to it."[27]

---

nisi cum domini proprii conscientia. Praetereuntem vero haec decrevimus extra communionem esse, ne nomen domini blasphemetur. Convenit vero civitatis episcopo, curam solicitudinemque necessariam monasteriis exhibere."—C. of Chalcedon (451) c. 4—Harduin, II, 601.

[25] "Clerici in ptochiis (domus mendicorum) et in monasteriis aut martyriis constituti, sub potestate sint ejus, qui in ea est civitate episcopus."—C. of Chalcedon (451), c. 8—Harduin, II, 601.

[26] ". . . monasterii vero omnis laica multitudo ad curam abbatis pertineat: neque ex ea sibi episcopus quidquam vindicet: aut aliquem ex illa clericum, nisi, abbate petente, praesumat. Hoc enim et rationis et religionis plenum est, ut clerici ad ordinationem episcopi debita subjectione respiciant: laica vero omnis monasterii congregatio ad solam ac liberam abbatis proprii quem sibi ipsi elegerit, ordinationem dispositionemque pertineat; regula, quae a fundatore ipsius monasterii dudum constituta est, in omnibus custodita."—C. of Arles (455)—Harduin, II, 781.

[27] "Quae semel ex voluntate episcopi dedicata sunt monasteria, perpetuo manere monasteria; et res quae ad ea pertinent, monasterio reservari."—C. of Chalcedon (451)—Harduin, II, 601.

The real importance of the Council of Chalcedon in regard to religious institutes seems to lie in the fact that by obliging the founders of monasteries to obtain the permission of the local ordinary, it thereby made of the monastery a strictly ecclesiastical institute, which one cannot say was the case before this. However, this only brings once more to the fore the question of ecclesiastical goods. If the monastery is an ecclesiastical organization, its possessions are ecclesiastical. And as the bishop is the administrator of all ecclesiastical goods in his diocese, his right extends over the goods of the monastery.

The logic of this is inescapable, but it seems quite certain that the case was not settled on logic. The monasteries continued to exercise control over their possessions, and not without some show of reason because even the Council of Chalcedon in canon 24, which has been cited, admitted: *"res quae ad ea pertinent monasterio reservari."* The Third Council of Arles, also mentioned above, declared: *"regula, quae a fundatore ipsius monasterii dudum constituta est, in omnibus custodita."* Now the rule of the founders entrusts the administration to the superior and officials, not to the bishop.

This question continued to be agitated; for it is found to be constantly recurring in the various councils. Thus, almost one hundred years later a certain Abbot Peter appeared before the Synod of Carthage of 525 claiming exemption for his monastery. The argument he advances is that the monastery had been built at the expense of the religious or their parents. On the strength of this he says to the Synod: *"Ideoque humiles supplicamus . . . a jugo nos clericorum, quod neque nobis neque patribus nostris, quisquam superponere aliquando tentavit, eruere digneris."* He then gives other arguments from St. Augustine (Book II, *de moribus clericorum*), and from the decree of the Third Council of Arles, already cited. In answer to this petition it pleased the Synod to use the very strong words: *"Erunt igitur omnia omnino monasteria, sicut semper fuerunt, a conditione clericorum modis omnibus libera, sibi tantum et Deo placentia.*"[28]

This decree was reaffirmed a few years later by the Council of Carthage of 534. Referring to the same monastery mentioned above the Council decreed: "*De monasterio abbatis Petri . . . quae universali concilio . . . acta sunt, inconvulsa permaneant.*" But then, concerning monasteries in general, the Council had this to say:

> Cetera vero monasteria etiam ipsa libertate plenissima perfruantur; servatis limitibus conciliorum suorum in haec dumtaxat, ut quandocumque voluerint sibi clericos ordinare, vel oratoria monasteriis dedicare, episcopus in cujus plebe, vel civitate locus monasterii consistit, ipse hujus muneris gratiam compleat, salva libertate monachorum: nihil in eis praeter hanc ordinationem vindicans, neque ecclesiasticis eos conditionibus, aut angariis subdens. . . .[29]

Other councils, it is true, have somewhat different legislation regarding the power of the bishop over the monastery. However, there seems to be no council that expressly gives to the bishop control over monastic property, whilst many deny this control.[30]

From these decrees, then, it seems quite certain that the right of the bishop as diocesan administrator was in practice and by conciliar law suspended in the case of religious institutes. Many authors see in the legislation here cited the beginning of the privilege of exemption.[31]

---

[28] Synod of Carthage (525)—Harduin, II, 1087.

[29] C. of Carthage (534)—Harduin, II, 1177.

[30] Besides the councils mentioned above, cf. C. of Lerida (584), c. 3—*MPL,* LXXXIV, 323; C. of Toledo (671), c. 51—*MPL,* LXXXIV, 378; C. of St. Agatha (544), c. 56—*MPL,* LXXXIV, 271; this council seems to give the bishop the right of supervision over the abbot's administration.

[31] Bouix, *De Jure Regularium,* P. V, c. II; Wernz, *Jus Decretalium,* n. 701; Zaccarias, *Antifebronius,* P. II, lib. V, c. 1.

PAPAL LEGISLATION.—It can hardly be denied that Pope St. Gregory the Great granted the right of electing the abbot and control over their temporal goods to practically all monasteries. Not only his letter to Marinianus of Ravenna, but also his letters to Bishop Castorius and to Abbot Luminosus make this practically certain.[32] At the same time it is worthy of remark that not only the thought, but even the words in these letters reecho strongly the Council of Carthage of 534, showing Gregory's sympathy with, if not approbation of, this Council.[33] Where the Pontiff decreed otherwise than here stated, it seems to have been for special reasons. Thus in Epistle 40 of Book I he appoints a certain bishop Paulinus as abbot of a monastery. But, as Gregory states, the monastery is *patrimonii nostri.* At the same time there is no superior there and apparently very few monks. In Epistle 59 of Book I he appoints an administrator for the temporal goods of the monastery of St. Lucy in Sicily; but the *"Abbas Joannes plurima se monasterii sui asserit habere negotia."*[34]

After Gregory the control of the monasteries over their temporal goods became an established fact as far as the Church Law was concerned. In fact, the Holy See in many cases granted complete exemption to certain monasteries. To explain this it is necessary to keep in mind that the early councils already cited, as well as the letters of Pope St. Gregory, look upon the freedom of the monastery from episcopal control in internal affairs as a matter of right and justice. But from the time of Pope St. Gregory to the thirteenth century the power of the bishop was in many cases not only ecclesiastical but also temporal. Likewise the monastic possessions became much larger because of grants of lands from bishops and princes. To protect the monasteries not only from the encroachments of secular princes, but even from the bishops, the Holy See began to take them under

[32] *MPL,* LXXVII, 918, 578, 580.

[33] Cf. also *Epistolae Gregorii Magni—MPL,* LXXVII, 458, 660, 832, 917.

[34] *MPL,* LXXVII, 493, 525.

its special protection. Thus, the Monastery of Bobbio in 633 received exemption from Pope Honorius I.[35] Under Nicholas I in the ninth century exemptions were numerous.[36] In the eleventh century Pope Leo IX confirmed the privileges granted the abbot of Cluny, which exempted him from the spiritual and temporal jurisdiction of the bishop and secular authorities. *"Nec ullus sive imperator, sive rex, vel archiepiscopus vel episcopus aliquam in aliquo potestatem exercere praesumat."*[37] Pope Urban II in 1090 granted exemption to the Monastery of Vallombrosa.[38] Even the First Council of the Lateran of 1123, which subjected some of the external activities of the monks to the control of the bishop, left untouched their free control of temporal goods.[39]

Thus, freedom in the administration of temporal goods can be put down as Church Law for monastic institutes from the sixth century till the Council of Trent. The exceptions to this rule seem to have been: 1. That in certain cases, where the laws of foundation so decreed, an account of administration had to be given to the founder or to a civil officer, or to the bishop; 2. monasteries of nuns, because of the inexperience of the members, were not infrequently administered or at least supervised by the bishop or by a regular superior, or by lay-administrators; 3. by apostolic indult a portion of the revenues of certain monasteries was granted *in commendam* to individuals who were not members of the institute; 4. certain goods entrusted to the religious, but intended for the parish or a pious work or mission, as well as the execution of pious wills and testaments, were subject to the supervision of the local ordinary.[40]

---

[35] *MPL*, LXXXVII, 1063.

[36] Melo, *De Exemptione Regularium*, p. 10.

[37] Lyszczarczyk, *Compendium Privilegiorum Regularium*, p. 35

[38] Urban II, *"Cum universi"*—Petra, *In Const. Apost.*, I, 187.

[39] I C. of Lateran (1123)—Mansi, XXI, 281 ff.

[40] C. 31, X, *de praebendis et dignit.*, III, 5; c. 3, X, *de dom. rel.*, III, 36; c. 17, X, *de test. et ult. vol.*, III, 26; c. un., *de test. et ult. vol.*, III, 6 in Clem.

The Council of Trent recognizing the long standing right of the religious institutes to control over their temporal goods said: "But the administration of the property of monasteries, or of convents, shall belong to the officers thereof only, removable at the will of their superiors."[41] But realizing that this was impossible where the revenues had been granted *in commendam* to persons not belonging to the institute or order, it states a wish in Session XXV:

> . . . that the most holy Roman Pontiff will, of his piety and prudence, make it his care, as far as he sees that the times will permit, that over those monasteries which are at present held *in commendam,* and which are conventual, there be appointed regulars, expressly professed of the same order, and capable of guiding and governing the flock. And as to such as shall become vacant hereafter, they shall be conferred solely on regulars of distinguished virtue and holiness. But as regards those monasteries which are the heads and chiefs of orders . . . those who hold them at present *in commendam* shall be bound . . . either to make, within six months a solemn profession of the religious life which is peculiar to the said order, or to resign. . . .[42]

Even the right of nuns to freedom in internal administration was recognized by the Holy Synod, especially when they were governed by their own chapters or by regular superiors. In other cases they were subject to the bishop as delegate of the Holy See.[43]

Legislation on the administration of temporal goods in monastic orders of men became fixed at the Council of Trent and has remained so ever since. It is repeated by the Code, which, however, states in canon 533 § 1, 4° that to invest or change the investment of money given for a parish or a mission, even regular administrators need permission of the local ordinary; and

---

[41] C. of Trent, Sess. XXV, *de reg.*, c. 2.

[42] C. of Trent, Sess. XXV, *de reg.*, c. 21.

[43] *Ibid.* c. 9.

likewise the administration of these funds is subject to his supervision.[44]

Administration in Monasteries of Nuns.—As has been seen, monasteries of nuns as well as those of men enjoyed in some cases the privilege of exemption by which they were subject only to the Holy See. As it is evident that the Holy See could not watch over each and all of these convents, especially when independent and not connected with a congregation or order, the Council of Trent[45] ordered that all such convents should group together into congregations and be governed by general chapters. Until this was done such convents were placed under the government of the local bishop, who was the delegate of the Holy See.[46] However, it was impossible to make this legislation immediately effective, and in many cases old customs were continued; although the bishops from time to time made efforts to use their delegated powers.[47] In 1622 Pope Gregory XV in his celebrated constitution "*Inscrutabili*" made a determined effort to remedy all these customs which were now really abuses.[48] He even extended the law which subjected the nuns to the local ordinary and decreed that henceforth all monasteries of nuns, even those subject to regulars, were, in temporal as in spiritual matters, subject to the local ordinary who would act as the delegate of the Holy See. In virtue of this law the administrators of such convents were obliged to render to the bishop a yearly report of their administration and were liable to penalties for mal-administration.

This constitution became the permanent law for the administration of temporal goods in convents of nuns, as later popes who legislated on this matter did nothing more than confirm the

---

[44] Canon 535 § 3,2°.

[45] Sess. XXV, *de reform.*, c. 8.

[46] *Ibid.* c. 9.

[47] Cf. S.C.Ep. et Reg., *Spoletana*, 17 July 1754—*Fontes*, n. 1313; S.C.Ep. et Reg., *Placentina*, 25 May 1575—*Fontes*, n. 1324; S.C.Ep. et Reg., *Spalatin*, 9 March 1593—*Fontes*, n. 1478.

[48] Gregory XV, const. "*Inscrutabili*," 5 Feb. 1622—*Fontes*, n. 199.

laws of Pope Gregory.[49] This does not mean, however, that full compliance with the law became the rule immediately. Benedict XIV confesses: *"easdem pontificum sanctiones usu minime receptas esse, neque executione unquam demandatas, uti plurimorum annorum experientia cognovimus."*[50] But he admits that the decisions of the Roman Congregations were uniform in enforcing this law.

The Code in canon 535 § 1 repeated this legislation governing the temporal goods of nuns, and in canon 533 § 1 made it of obligation for them to get permission of the local ordinary for all investments or change of investments.

Administration in Congregations of Simple Vows.—Till the middle of the sixteenth century the vows taken in religious institutes of men were solemn and it was forbidden by the Church to take what are now known as simple vows. By his apostolic constitution *"Lubricum vitae genus,"* Pope Pius V in 1568 ordered the superiors of every group living in common without solemn vows to have all subjects declare within twenty-four hours after receiving notice whether they wished to make solemn profession or not. Those unwilling to do so were to return to the world. The rest were given one month's time in which to hold a meeting and decide which of the then approved rules they would adopt.[51]

This law, it seems, applied only to those who called themselves religious; which explains how the Congregation of St. Philip Neri, founded by him in 1566, received permission to continue as a congregation from Gregory XIII in 1575, and had its rules approved by Paul V in 1612. Though the members of this society lived in common under obedience, they took no vows, nor

---

[49] Cf. Clement XII, const. *"Admonet nos,"* 11 Aug. 1735—*Fontes*, n. 297; Benedict XIV, const. *"Ad militantis,"* 30 March 1742—*Fontes*, n. 326; Clement XIII, const. *"Inter multiplices,"* 11 Dec. 1758—*Fontes*, n. 449.

[50] *Institutiones*, XXIX, n. 5.

[51] Pius V, const. *"Lubricum vitae genus,"* 17 Nov. 1568—*Bull. Rom.*, VII, 725.

did they call themselves religious.[52] The law of Pius V, however, did not remain long in force, for in 1593 a religious congregation of simple vows applied to Pope Clement VIII for approval of their constitutions and approval was granted. But in 1621 Pope Gregory XV changed the vows from simple to solemn.[53] Similar to this was the Congregation of the Bethlehemites. Approved as a congregation with simple vows by Innocent XI in 1687[54] the institute was later changed to an order with solemn vows by Clement XI.[55]

Meanwhile, in 1624 St. Vincent de Paul had founded his Congregation of the Mission. They lived in community and pronounced vows. But although their institute was approved by Urban VIII in 1632, the vows pronounced by the members were not accepted in the name of the Church.[56] Other congregations of a similar nature were established in the course of time. However, for the reason that the vows of the members were not public, these congregations are not religious institutes in the strict sense of the term.[57]

It was not until the eighteenth century that approval was given to religious congregations that have retained that name even under the Code. By an apostolic rescript of 18 April 1746 Pope Benedict XIV approved the rules of the Passionists founded by St. Paul of the Cross in 1725. In 1769 Pope Clement XIV confirmed this approval of the rules.[58] In 1732 St. Alphonsus Maria de Liguori founded the Congregation of the Most Holy Redeemer. The rules and the institute founded by

---

[52] Ingold, "Oratory of St. Philip Neri," *Cath. Encycl.*, XI, 272.

[53] Gregory XV, const. *"In supremo apostolatus,"* 3 Nov. 1621—*Bull. Rom.*, XII, 608.

[54] Const. *"Ecclesiae catholicae,"* 26 March 1687—*Bull. Rom.*, XIX, 735.

[55] Const. *"Ex debito pastorali,"* 3 April 1710—*Bull. Rom.*, XXI, 385.

[56] Const. *"Salvatoris nostri,"* 12 Jan. 1632—"Congregation of the Mission," *Cath. Encycl.*, X, 358.

[57] Cf. canon 488,1°.

[58] Litt. apos. *"Supremi apostolatus,"* 15 Nov. 1769—*Bull. Rom. Cont.*, III, 105.

St. Alphonsus were approved by Pope Benedict XIV on February 25, 1749.[59] Other congregations of simple vows soon followed and received the approval of the Holy See. In fact, it is now the custom of the Holy See to approve new institutes not as orders but only as congregations.

As to the administration of the temporal goods in these institutes, there was at first no Church law directly applicable to them. The founders drew up rules and constitutions which were followed by the members, and these constitutions contained the details of administration. But in this form the constitutions could be changed by the members in chapter or by the local ordinaries. When, however, the constitutions were approved by the Holy See, they became particular papal law for the institute. In the rescript of approval it was usually stated whether or not the institute was subject to the local ordinary or exempt from his jurisdiction. Thus the laws governing each institute varied and there was no uniformity till the constitution "*Conditae a Christo*" was promulgated by Pope Leo XIII in 1900. But before considering this document, consideration will be given to congregations of women with simple vows.

The members of religious institutes for women originally took the same vows as the male religious and were usually affiliated with the first order. In 1521, however, Pope Leo X approved and confirmed a Third Order of Franciscans with simple vows.[60] Whether or not this approbation was recognized by the Council of Trent cannot now be ascertained. At any rate the Council of Trent, without mentioning this congregation, renewed the law of Boniface VIII and enjoined on all bishops the restoration of the enclosure of nuns (hence solemn vows) wherever it had been violated.[61] However, if the Council of Trent passed over the existence of this congregation of simple vows, Pope Pius V, in his

---

[59] Litt. Ap. "*Ad pastoralis*"—*Constitutiones et Regulae C.Ss.R.* (1929), p. 33.

[60] Const. "*Inter cetera,*" 20 Jan. 1521—*Bull. Rom.*, V, 764.

[61] Council of Trent, Sess. XXV, *de reg.*, c. 5.

constitution "*Circa Pastoralis,*"[62] made it clear that such institutes were abolished and declared that in future no third order of regulars would be recognized unless they pronounced solemn vows and observed the law of enclosure. In order not to subject the nuns thus enclosed to special hardships, the Pontiff ordered the bishops and the superiors of such monasteries to have *conversae* or externs who were not professed, or if professed were at least forty years of age, to collect the alms of the faithful for the support of the nuns. If this was not sufficient other pious persons were to be used in this work, and the nuns themselves were permitted to do work within the monastery that would be a help towards their support. Finally, it was forbidden to superiors to receive into the convent more nuns than the revenues would support.[63]

But even this was not sufficient to abolish sisterhoods of simple vows, for as Benedict states,[64] it is certain that even after this decree of the Pope there were sisters living in many cities of Italy who had neither solemn vows nor observed enclosure. In order that the papal decrees might be upheld, these congregations were treated by the Holy See as if non-existent. However, it was impossible not to make some provision for their welfare and thus, by custom, the local bishop took charge of them.

It was not long, however, till the Holy See began to acknowledge their existence and to approve their rules though not their institutes. Benedict XIV, commenting on the approval of the rule of the 'English Ladies' by Clement XI, says that the approval of the rules was accompanied by the 'usual' clause denying approval to the institute.[65] If the clause was 'usual' the approbation of the rules of such institutes must antedate the year 1703.

---

[62] 29 May 1566—*Fontes*, n. 112.

[63] *Ibid.* nn. 5, 7.

[64] *Institutiones*, XXIX, n. 13.

[65] Benedict XIV, const. *"Quamvis justo,"* 30 April 1749—*Fontes*, n. 398.

Benedict himself 'tolerated' the foundations made by the English Ladies but continued to deny them approval of their institute for the reason that they lacked solemn vows, and therefore their existence was contrary to the laws of Boniface VIII and Pius V.[66] At the same time he makes it clear that institutes of such a character are subject to the local ordinary. Thus in section XIX of this constitution he says that the superioress may visit the houses but must afterwards report on them to the bishop. She may transfer members "with permission of the local ordinaries." In fact, the idea given is that the real superior is the bishop and not the one chosen from among the members of the institute, since in section XX he says that the authority of the bishop is maintained without the necessity of abolishing the office of superioress. This undoubtedly gave the bishop a large amount of control over the administration of temporalities. But how the administration was conducted cannot be determined since it is not mentioned by Pope Benedict. However, the rules undoubtedly regulated the details of administration, and since they at least were approved, they had the force of particular law.

In 1819 papal approval was given for the first time to an institute of women of simple vows. This occurred in the case of the Sisters of Charity. Their rule had been approved in 1816,[67] and three years later Pope Pius VII approved not only the rule but the institute.[68] At the same time he abrogated the former laws prohibiting institutes of simple vows.

From this time on many institutes of men and women which professed only simple vows were founded. Some received the approbation of the Holy See; some only that of the local ordinary. Though it is true that the rules and constitutions when approved by the Holy See were particular law for each institute, still, as Pope Leo XIII remarked, there were some of the opinion that the rights and duties of the bishop in regard to

---

[66] *Ibid.* n. XXIII.

[67] *Acta Pii VII,* II, 1227.

[68] Const. "*Dominici Gregis,*" 14 Dec. 1819—*Acta Pii VII,* II, 1990.

these institutes were uncertain and controverted.[69] To clear up the doubts Pope Leo on December 8, 1900 issued his constitution "*Conditae a Christo,*" a document which has been called the 'charter' of religious congregations.

Pope Leo divided these congregations into two classes: 1. Diocesan institutes, those which exist only in virtue of episcopal authority; 2. Pontifical institutes, those which have received at least a papal decree of commendation.

Of the temporal administration in diocesan institutes Pope Leo disposed in a very few words: "*Episcopus ius habet . . . de oeconomicis rationibus cognoscendi.*"[70] In view of the rest of the document there is more in this sentence than would at first appear. Except when the institute was clerical,[71] the Pope did not expressly grant to the superiors of the institute the right to administer temporalities, as he did to superiors of pontifical institutes.[72] Then, too, the constitutions of diocesan institutes were approved solely by the bishop, and as long as the institute had not extended beyond his diocese he had the power to change them. For these reasons it seems that the bishop could determine the officials for administration, the manner of administration, what was ordinary administration and what extraordinary, and so forth. Once these things were determined, however, it was probably expected that the bishop would leave the acts of administration to the various officials, reserving to himself the right to examine the accounts or to give permission for certain acts.

In pontifical institutes more power was granted to the superiors and less to the bishop. In the first place the officials were appointed by the chapter. Though the bishop had the right to preside at such chapters if the institute was one of women, he did so, not of his own authority, but as the delegate of the Holy

---

[69] Leo XIII, const. "*Conditae a Christo,*" 8 Dec. 1900—*Fontes*, n. 644.

[70] *Ibid.* Ch. I, n. X.

[71] *Ibid.* Ch. II, n. XI.

[72] *Ibid.* Ch. II, n. IX.

See. Moreover, it is not stated here, as it was for diocesan institutes, that he had the right to confirm or rescind the election.[73]

The administration of the goods of the institute was in the hands of the highest superior; whilst the revenues of each house were administered by the local superior. The bishop was not allowed to demand an account of this administration. However, if any property was contributed or willed to a particular house to be used in that place for divine worship or charitable purposes, the administration of it was to be conducted by the superior. In his administration, however, the superior was entirely subject to the bishop, who could examine the accounts as often as he wished and take care that the capital was not lessened nor the revenues ill-spent.[74] In regard to schools, asylums, etc., conducted by pontifical institutes, the bishop had the same rights as he had over the houses.[75] However, in regard to all these laws Pope Leo made it clear that they did not revoke former faculties or privileges granted by the Holy See or confirmed by centenary or immemorial custom or contained in rules and constitutions approved by the Holy See.

Heretofore the Holy See merely examined the rules that were submitted to it and usually left the details to the person or persons establishing the institute. In 1901, however, the Sacred Congregation of Bishops and Regulars issued a set of '*Normae.*' These were to serve as a model for the constitutions of all future religious congregations. These norms reiterated all the regulations of the constitution "*Conditae a Christo*" regarding temporal administration, and in addition stated that a report containing a financial statement should be sent to the Holy See every three years.[76] In the case of institutes of women, the bishop of the place where the mother-house was located first examined this report in order to attest to its truthfulness. Be-

[73] *Ibid.* Ch. II, nn. I, IX.

[74] *Ibid.* Ch. II, n. IX.

[75] *Ibid.* Ch. II, n. XI.

[76] *Normae secundum quas S.Cong. Ep. et Reg. procedere solet in approbandis novis institutis votorum simplicium,* 28 June 1907, n, 262.

cause of this it may be said that the *Normae* introduced the obligation now contained in the Code, whereby institutes of women, even of pontifical right, have to submit the account of their administration to the bishop before sending it to the Holy See.[77] However, as much of the information required by the Holy See was at times omitted from these reports, the Sacred Congregation of Bishops and Regulars sent out a decree which obliged the supreme moderators to answer every three years a set form of questions on matters in which were included acts of administration.[78] Apart from this there was no change made in the legislation on temporal administration.

A change did come, however, in 1909. Because of the "too great facility with which debts were contracted," the Sacred Congregation of Religious issued an instruction[79] to all religious institutes, whereby the various superiors were forbidden for the future to contract any notable debts without the previous consent of their consultors and respective higher superiors in the various cases. Notable sums were defined as: Over five hundred to one thousand lire for a house; over one thousand to five thousand lire for a province; over five thousand to ten thousand lire for the general curia. For sums over ten thousand lire, besides the other necessary permissions, it was also necessary to obtain the '*beneplacitum apostolicum.*'[80] The Code allowed debts to the amount of thirty thousand lire ($6,000) to be contracted before making it necessary to obtain the permission of the Holy See, and linked the laws for alienations with those for debts and obligations.[81]

Besides these regulations regarding debts. the Instruction obliged all institutes to appoint consultors or chapters as aids to the various superiors in their administration.[82] It defined

---

[77] *Ibid.* n. 262; cf. can. 510.

[78] S.C.Ep. et Reg., decretum, July 16, 1906—*Fontes,* n. 2052.

[79] "*Inter ea,*" July 30, 1909—*Fontes,* n. 4394.

[80] *Ibid.* n. 1.

[81] Canon 534.

[82] *Ibid.* n. II.

the rights and duties of these consultors in regard to the goods of the moral person, investments, Mass stipends, dowries, and so forth.[83] It forbade new buildings or extensive repairs if the money had to be borrowed for these purposes. In particular, it stated that where constitutions and rules were stricter than the Instruction itself, they were still to be followed; but if opposed to the Instruction they were abrogated. If the institute had no constitutions on temporal goods, constitutions were to be formulated as soon as possible and according to the '*Normae*' of 1901, chapter VI, and the tenor of the Instruction, "*Inter ea.*"[84]

The Code in 1918 confirmed existing legislation on temporal administration with slight changes. Thus, for investing money or changing an investment the superioress of nuns or of diocesan sisters must have the permission of the local ordinary.[85] As already mentioned, the amount of a debt that could be contracted without obtaining the permission of the Holy See was increased from ten thousand to thirty thousand lire.[86] The report to the Holy See was to be sent every five years instead of every three years.[87] Finally, some additions were made to the legislation regarding the responsibility for debts contracted by the institute or its members.[88]

After the Code the Sacred Congregation of Religious issued a decree stating that the obligation of the Code regarding the quinquennial report, as stated in canon 510, was incumbent upon moderators of all institutes of pontifical right without exception.[89] A few days later it issued a list of questions, similar to

---

[83] S.C.deRel., instr. "*Inter ea,*" July 30, 1909, nn. V, VII, VIII, IX, XI, XII—*Fontes,* n. 4394.

[84] *Ibid.* n. X.

[85] Canon 533 § 1,1°.

[86] Canon 534 § 1.

[87] Canon 510.

[88] Canon 536.

[89] Decretum, March 8, 1922, n. IV—*AAS,* XIV (1922), 161.

those of 1906, to be answered in this report. But these made no changes in temporal administration.[90]

Article II. Commentary

CANON 532

§ 1. "*Bona tum religionis, tum provinciae domusque, administrentur ad normam constitutionum.*

§ 2. *Expensas et actus juridicos ordinariae administrationis valide, praeter Superiores, faciunt, intra fines sui muneris, officiales quoque, qui in constitutionibus ad hoc designantur.*"

Paragraph 1 of this canon states a general rule for the administration of religious ecclesiastical property, viz., whatever the constitutions prescribe for the administration of property should be observed. The Code here presupposes: 1. That the institute, province, and house have each separate capacity to own property;[91] 2. That the constitutions contain norms for the administration of property.[92]

Paragraph 2 of canon 532 states a general rule for ordinary administration: The act is always valid if the superior or official who performs it does not exceed his powers of office. It will be seen that certain formalities are sometimes required even in the performance of acts of ordinary administration, e. g., the permission of a higher superior, a permission in writing, etc. In virtue of the general rule stated in this paragraph, such formalities concern only the liceitness of the act not its validity, unless this is expressly stated, as in canon 1530 § 1,3°.

---

[90] S.C. de Rel., instr. March 25, 1922—*AAS*, XV (1923), 459.

[91] If ownership is forbidden by the constitutions or rules to any or all of these units, administrative acts, when necessary, are performed in virtue of delegated power.

[92] The instruction *"Inter ea"* of the S.C. de Rel. imposed on religious institutes the obligation to insert norms for temporal administration in their constitutions where such were lacking. Cf. S.C. de Rel, instr. *"Inter ea,"* 30 July 1909, n. X—*Fontes*, n. 4394.

1. DEFINITION OF ADMINISTRATION.

Administration or administrative power is a part of the executive branch of the government. In a general way the function of an executive is to remove all obstacles that are a hindrance to the attainment of the proper end of the society. The executive's duties are threefold: 1. To direct and govern the members; 2. To care for and administer the means which the society possesses for attaining its end; 3. To oblige the members to work towards the attainment of that end. These duties are sometimes signified by the one word 'administration.' In its strict sense, however, administration is concerned not with the members of a society, but with the means which a society has for attaining its end.[93] In this sense administration may be defined as the care and preservation of those means which are necessary or useful for attaining the proper end of a society.[94] But as such a definition extends itself not only to temporal goods but also to all spiritual, moral, and intellectual factors which are necessary or useful for a society, it exceeds the scope of this treatise. To suit the purposes of canon 532, administration is defined as: The control or care of the temporal goods of a religious institute, in order that they may serve the purposes for which they were acquired. This definition includes all acts which are necessary or useful: 1. To keep property in good condition; 2. To make it productive; 3. To derive benefit from it; 4. To apply, pay out, and use it for legitimate purposes.[95]

---

[93] Ottaviani, *Institutiones Juris Pub. Eccl.*, I, 120.

[94] Even the acquisition of property has been included under ecclesiastical administration in its wide sense. Cf. S.C.P.F., 21 July 1856—*Collectanea*, I, n. 1127; S.C.C., litt. *Ad omnes Ordinarios Italiae*, 20 June 1929, art. 41—*AAS*, XXI (1929), 394; Wernz, *Jus Decret.*, III, n. 147.

[95] Larraona, "Commentarium Codicis," *CpR*, XII (1931), 355, 356; Vromant, *De Bonis Eccl. Temp.*, n. 172; Wernz, *Jus Decretalium*, III, n. 147; Vermeersch-Creusen, *Epitome*, I, n. 841.

2. DIVISION OF ADMINISTRATION.

Since administration is the care of temporal things, it is clear that the acts of administration will be many and diverse. The upkeep and improvement of property will entail one class of acts; the perception of income, another; the payment of debts and the settlement of claims, a third. In general all these acts, in so far as they are or are not subject to civil laws or formalities, will be *juridical* or *non juridical* acts. This distinction, however, is of no great importance in canon law except to stress the fact that the Code commands the observance of civil laws and formalities in administration in general, and in particular in negotiating contracts and payments that involve church property, unless the law or formalities are contrary to the divine or ecclesiastical law.[96]

The important distinction in regard to administrative acts is whether they are acts of *ordinary* administration or acts of *extraordinary* administration. This is important because superiors and designated officials act validly in performing acts of ordinary administration; whereas for acts of extraordinary administration they need a special faculty.

ORDINARY ADMINISTRATION.—Ordinary administration, considered in the acts of administration, includes all those acts which are regularly necessary for the upkeep of property and for supplying current needs.[97] Ordinary administration, considered in the administrator, i. e., the superior, or designated official, includes all those acts which the administrator may validly perform in virtue of his office.

It is easy enough, as a rule, to determine what acts are *regularly* necessary. Thus, the collecting of debts that are paid in regular installments; the collecting of rentals for houses and lands; the perception of annual, semi-annual, or quarterly interest or dividends; the purchase of supplies needed for daily use;

[96] Canons 1523,2°; 1529.

[97] Larraona, "Commentarium Codicis," *CpR,* XII (1931), 356.

the sale of crops or other perishable produce; the banking of money for purposes of security or convenience; and other similar acts, are all *per se* acts of ordinary administration, because *regularly necessary.*[98] In particular cases, however, the above mentioned acts are not acts of ordinary administration, unless the administrator who performs the act is competent *ex officio* to do so. In view of this it is impossible to state precisely which acts are extraordinary for this or that particular administrator. This can only be determined after learning the extent of the power conferred on the administrator in question by the Code or by the particular law of his religious institute.[99] Sometimes the particular law is explicit in determining the powers of the various administrators; sometimes it states only general norms, leaving the details to the superiors.

Even when an act is regularly necessary the law may consider it of such importance as to require administrators in general, or at least certain administrators, to obtain a superior's previous permission or to observe some other formality before performing the act. The performance of other acts, not beyond the administrator's competence, but perhaps not regularly necessary, may likewise oblige the administrator to obtain a previous permission or observe other formalities. In all such cases, if the administrator omits nothing that is essential to the act or expressly prescribed for validity, the act is valid even though the permission or formalities have been omitted. This is evident from the Code which states that acts of ordinary administration are *validly* performed by superiors and designated officials unless they exceed the powers of their office.[100] Particular law may determine that certain acts are extraordinary even though in common law they are ordinary. But the common law principle that the validity of an act depends only on essentials and on for-

---

[98] Vromant, *De Bonis Eccl. Temp.*, n. 173.

[99] Larraona, "Commentarium Codicis," *CpR,* XII (1931), 356.

[100] Canons 532 § 2; 1680 § 1; Larraona, "Commentarium Codicis," *CpR,* XII (1931), 357; Berutti, *Institutiones J.C.*, III, 116.

malities expressly prescribed for validity, holds also for particular law.[101]

Extraordinary Administration.—In general extraordinary administration includes all those acts which are beyond the power of the administrator and for the performance of which he needs a special faculty or permission not included in his office. Like ordinary administration, the exact concept of extraordinary administration is juridical and its determination depends in particular cases on the rank of the administrator and the constitutions of his religious institute. In accordance with the importance of the act, religious particular law determines it to be of ordinary or of extraordinary administration, and prescribes the faculties, permissions, or formalities that are required for its performance. The Canon Law of the Church mentions without specifying ordinary and extraordinary administration. However, when speaking of acts which exceed ordinary administration the Code declares them invalid unless the faculty (*facultas*) to perform them has been obtained; or if it uses the word permission (*licentia*), it states expressly that this is necessary for validity.[102] When speaking of acts of ordinary administration it sometimes requires for their performance a previous permission, but without using the word '*facultas*' or stating that the permission is for the validity of the act.[103]

The acts of extraordinary administration are principally those by which the capital of the moral person is disposed of. Thus, alienations of property by selling, giving away, exchanging, and by contracts "by which the condition of the moral person may become less secure," such as going bond or security, giving a lien or mortgage, contracting debts and obligations, borrowing, leasing church property for more than nine years.[104] Other acts

[101] Canon 1680 § 1; Vromant, *op. cit.*, n. 173.

[102] Cf. canons 1527 § 1; 1530 § 1,3°; 1532 § 4.

[103] Cf. canons 1523,4°; 1526; 1536 § 2; Larraona, "Commentarium Codicis," *CpR*, XII (1931), 357; Vromant, *De Bonis Eccl. Temp.*, n. 172 bis.

[104] Cf. canons 534; 1538; 1541.

can and do come under the classification of extraordinary administration. The determination of these is left to the various rules and constitutions.[105]

3. NORMS OF ADMINISTRATION.

Canon 532 § 1 states that the property of the institute, province, and house should be administered according to the norms of the constitutions. This supposes that the constitutions of the various religious institutes have norms for the administration of temporal goods. Actually there should be no difficulty on this score, since religious institutes in existence before 1909 were obliged by the instruction *Inter ea* to formulate norms for the administration of temporal goods if such norms were lacking in their constitutions. The model to be followed was the instruction itself and the "*Normae*" of 1901, chapter VI.[106] Institutes founded since 1909 would probably be required to comply with n. 23 of the "*Normae*" of 1921, and to have a section in their revised constitutions treating of "government, administration, and offices."[107]

The details of administration in regard to the manner of performing certain acts, the administrator authorized to perform them, and so forth, are as a rule carefully set down and regulated in the constitutions. For this reason the Code, even in those canons which treat of administration, usually refers to the constitutions in regard to the details of administration, and confirms the constitutions in so far as they are not contrary to the Code. If details are mentioned in the Code, it is usually only when the intervention of an authority external to the institute is necessary for performing an act.[108]

---

[105] Cf. Vromant, *De Bonis Eccl. Temp.*, n. 173.

[106] S.C. de Rel., instr. "*Inter ea*," July 3, 1909, n. X—*Fontes*, n. 4394.

[107] *Normae secundum quas S.C. de Rel., in novis religiosis congregationibus approbandis procedere solet*, Romae, 1922, Ch. V.

[108] Canon 489; Larraona, *op. cit.*, XII (1931), 355, 356.

There are, however, certain fundamental norms that the Church always insists upon in the administration of ecclesiastical property. These norms should be observed in administering religious ecclesiastical property:

1. The will of the faithful who have donated or left property to pious causes should be carried out exactly. "It is an accepted principle that the first thing to be considered is the will of the donor."[109]

2. The ecclesiastical patrimony should be conserved as far as possible.[110]

3. Law suits and abuse of administrative power should be avoided.[111]

4. There should be a plurality of administrators in all important matters, not indeed as to the actual carrying out of the act, but for the determination of its necessity, utility, etc. For this reason the Code obliges superiors to have the advice or consent of their consultors on many occasions.[112]

5. Higher superiors should always exercise supervision over the acts of inferior administrators. This supervision is necessary in particular cases of greater importance, and also generally, in the form of a yearly or quinquennial report.[113]

4. SUBJECTS OF ADMINISTRATION.

In canon 532 § 2 the superiors and the officials designated in the constitutions are indicated as the active subjects of ordinary administration. Strictly speaking there is no subject of extraordinary administration. This kind of administration pre-

---

[109] Leo XIII, const. *"Romanos Pontifices,"* 8 May 1881, n. 26—*Fontes,* n. 582.

[110] S.C.P.F., instr. *Ad Vic. Ap. Sin.*, 18 Oct. 1883, n. XIV—*Fontes,* n. 4903.

[111] *Ibid.* Cf. canon 2412,1°.

[112] Canon 516.

[113] Cf. canons 533; 534; 512; 510; S.C. de Rel., decretum, March 8, 1922, n. IV—*AAS,* XIV (1922), 161.

supposes a lack of power in the administrator who performs the act, and an application to a higher superior for the power or for delegation. When this is granted it is the inferior administrator who performs the act and not the higher superior who has given the faculty or delegation.

According to canon 532 administrators should be designated by the constitutions. These will determine the power of the administrator, and the superior in whom the right of supervision resides. The Holy See exercises supervision over the whole religious institute by means of the quinquennial report which is of obligation for all pontifical institutes whether of simple or solemn vows, by reason of canon 510, and in view of a Decree of the Sacred Congregation of Religious of 1922; and of obligation for all pontifical institutes of simple vows by reason of the Instruction of the Sacred Congregation of Religious of 1922.[114]

The Roman Pontiff.—Canon 499 § 1 states that all religious are subject to the Roman Pontiff as their supreme Superior; and canon 1518 states that the Roman Pontiff is the supreme administrator and dispenser of all ecclesiastical property. This, of course, includes religious ecclesiastical property. This supremacy, however, does not make the Roman Pontiff the owner or the possessor of ecclesiastical property.[115] He is the *mediate* administrator in the sense that the norms of administration are papal law if found in the Code or in approved constitutions; and if found alsewhere must at least be in conformity with the laws of the Code.[116] Moreover, as stated in canon 1499 § 2, the moral person holds ownership of acquired property under the supreme authority of the Apostolic See. If the necessity or proportionate utility of the Church require it, the Roman Pontiff can use or dispose of the property of ecclesiastical moral persons for the greater good of the Church.[117]

[114] S.C. de Rel., instr. March 25, 1922—*AAS*, XV (1923), 459; S.C. de Rel., decretum, March 8, 1922, n. IV—*AAS*, XIV (1922), 161.

[115] *Summa*, II-II, Q. 100, art. 1, ad 7; canon 1499 § 2.

[116] Cf. canons 489; 1495 § 2; 1499 § 2.

[117] Pejska, *Jus Canonicum Religiosorum*, p. 60.

The Local Ordinary.—An important phase of the administration of property by religious is that which deals with the authority of the local ordinary over that administration. Property acquired by religious is not by that very fact completely withdrawn from the authority of the local ordinary. Canon 1519 § 1 states that the local ordinary has the right to supervise the administration of all ecclesiastical property in his territory. This right is limited only when ecclesiastical property has been withdrawn from the local ordinary's jurisdiction. The canons under consideration in this dissertation define to a large extent the limitations on the authority of the local ordinary over the property of religious institutes; or better perhaps, the relation between the local ordinary and the religious administrator. Considering the careful preparation given to the redaction of the Code, one is safe in believing that all the authority which is granted to the local ordinary over property *actually acquired by religious moral persons* is found stated in these canons. However, elsewhere in the Code frequent laws are found that regulate the administrative acts of religious. Sometimes these laws are a fuller explanation of those contained in canons 531-537; sometimes they are concerned with property that is administered by religious but which is not religious ecclesiastical property. In any case this administration is not without its difficulties and problems; and moreover, an explanation of it is necessary here and there for the proper understanding of the canons which are under consideration in this work. For this reason these canons have been referred to in the commentary to the canons proper to this dissertation.

By the local ordinary is meant the Roman Pontiff, residential bishops, abbots or prelates *nullius*, and their vicars-general, and also administrators, vicars, and prefects apostolic. The Roman Pontiff has ordinary jurisdiction over the whole Church. The others have ordinary jurisdiction in their respective territories. Moreover, ordinary jurisdiction is acquired by disposition of law or by approved custom by one who takes the place of, or serves as a substitute for, one of the above-mentioned ordinaries.[118]

The authority of the local ordinary over ecclesiastical property belonging to or administered by religious, as expressed in different parts of the Code, is:

1. *The Right to Receive Accounts.*—Canon 535.

This entitles the local ordinary to examine, personally or by his delegate, documents, contracts, receipts of payments, and also the various books containing expenditures and income, in order that he may form a correct idea of the financial condition of the persons or places under his jurisdiction. The books must contain the proper and necessary account of administration without padding or alterations; and in number and method should conform to the custom of the country or diocese. A mere financial statement is not sufficient for an accounting. However, when the administrator has once satisfied the requirements of this accounting, he is not to be troubled again till the time for the next accounting shall have arrived except for a just and proportionate cause.[119]

2. *The Right to Give Consent*—Canon 533.

The consent of the local ordinary is usually required by certain administrators for the more important acts of administration, such as investments, change of investments, alienations, and the like. When it is necessary to obtain a previous consent, it is necessary also to give an account of the subsequent administration.

3. *The Right of Supervision*—Canons 630; 1519.

This includes the right to visit and demand accounts (Can. 1519 § 1), and to prescribe a prudent mode of administration, but only according to the norms of the Code (Can. 1519 § 2).

---

[118] Canon 198.

[119] S.R.R., 20 Feb. 1913—*S.R. Rotae Decisiones*, V (1913), Dec. XV, n. 5; Pallottini, *Collectio Resolutionum S.C.C.*, XV, "redditio rationum," nn. 57, 58, 63.

On the strength of this the ordinary of the place or the religious superior will be able to oblige the administrator:

a) To make an inventory of the property in the proper form (Can. 1522,2°,3°);

b) To keep and file instruments and documents of purchases and other contracts (Canons 375-377);

c) To make necessary repairs, and to apply the revenues received; to follow out directions and suggestions as to administration, saving, in what concerns the application of revenues, the intention of the donors and the rights due by common or particular law to the administrator.

Supervision implies the right to receive a report of the quantity and value of the property; to demand an account as to the safe investment and the faithful application of donations; to apply remedies for negligent or incompetent administration, either personally or through the competent superior according to the norms of law.[120] It does not include the right to determine the manner in which the income or alms or other property are to be expended; nor, *a fortiori,* the right to claim the total distribution or partial paying out of this property. These things belong only to the person on whom by law the administration devolves.[121]

SUPERIORS.—Canon 532 § 2 makes it clear that superiors have the right to perform acts of administration. "The word 'superiors,'" says Larraona, "was inserted in the Code to dispel any doubts about their capacity to perform administrative acts. Logically and practically the right to perform acts of administration is necessary for them. Administration is part of government. Though generally entrusted to officials, radically it cannot be denied to those who have the right to govern. Moreover, the faculty must be reserved to them of placing economic acts directly, at least in certain cases, as for example to remedy the

---

[120] Cf. canon 535 § 1,2°.

[121] Vromant, *De Bonis Eccl. Temp.*, nn. 174, 175; Fanfani, *De Jure Regularium*, n. 452.

negligence of an administrator or to repair an injury done by him, etc.''[122]

As a rule, however, superiors should not take upon themselves the administration of temporal affairs, since the higher obligation of the superior is the spiritual welfare of his subjects. Too great an interest in temporal concerns may result in a neglect of spiritual matters, and possibly, even in the loss of the respect of his community. A superior whose greatest concern is money cheapens his office.[123]

Apart from these reasons the Code expressly forbids major superiors from exercising the office of econome or procurator and allows this to local rectors only in case of necessity.[124] Yet, though above mere temporalities, it is the duty of the superior to see that the temporal necessities of the community and the work entrusted to it are not neglected by those in charge of them. For this reason the superior has always the right of vigilance and direction over minor officials.[125] He can require minor officials to obtain his previous permission for the performance of more important acts of ordinary administration. In this, however, due regard must be had to the constitutions; and as already stated, this permission regards only the licitness of the act, since he cannot declare invalid those acts which are of ordinary administration. For the performance of acts of extraordinary administration he can delegate the power to minor officials, provided that he have it himself. What acts are to be considered ordinary and what extraordinary must be determined by the constitutions.

OFFICIALS.—The officials are those who normally make expenditures and perform juridical acts of ordinary administration. Their duties and the method of their appointment are usually stated in the constitutions. As already noted, their acts

---

[122] "Commentarium Codicis," *CpR*, XI (1931), 358.

[123] Vromant, *De Bonis Eccl. Temp.*, n. 229 bis.

[124] Canon 516 § 3.

[125] Canon 516 § 2.

are always valid if they do not exceed the limits of their office, even though they omit certain prescribed formalities. For this omission they can be punished or deposed from office, but their acts are not invalidated.[126]

Minor officials are always under the vigilance and direction of the superior. This vigilance even extends to offices that are external to the institute, as, for example, that of pastor, or of parochial vicar.[127] But it should not contravene the Code or the constitutions.

The obligation arising from the Code to appoint an econome extends only to those moral persons which have capacity by the constitutions to acquire property.[128]

---

[126] Canon 532 § 2.

[127] Canons 516 § 2; 630 § 4.

[128] Larraona, "Commentarium Codicis," *CpR*, XII (1931), 354.

CHAPTER III

INVESTMENTS

Canon 533 defines the right and duty of the local ordinary in regard to the investment of ecclesiastical property in the possession of religious. The extent of this right is regulated: 1. By the quality of the religious, i. e., whether they are of diocesan or of pontifical right, or whether they are male or female; 2. By the nature of the property, i. e., whether it is for diocesan projects or for works peculiar to the religious institute. In the former case the right of the local ordinary (in some cases the regular superior), is based on the presumed inability of the religious to cope with the problems of investments. In the latter it is based on the interest which the local ordinary may have in an investment because of its bearing on projects under his jurisdiction.

1. NATURE OF INVESTMENTS.

By an investment is usually understood the conversion of wealth or resources from an unproductive form to a productive form. The intention of the investor is to acquire additional wealth by productively employing his present wealth. In this way he hopes to supply his present and future needs without decrease of his means of supplying the needs.

There are as many ways of investing money as there are of spending money, and altogether too many to be noted here with any profit. In general the investor gives up the possession of his money or wealth and sometimes also the title to it, depending on the nature of the investment. Thus, by investing in lands and buildings one changes one's form of wealth, hoping for a yearly income from the rental of the land or buildings; by investing in bonds and mortgages one lends money to a borrower, expecting a return of the money lent plus a remuneration in the form of interest or dividends; by investing in stocks one purchases a share of a business or industry, hoping to participate in the profits of the industry and, if necessary, regain the original investment by selling the shares in one's possession.

From this it may be seen that there is in most investments an element of risk. Even supposing the entire honesty of the business man or borrower or tenant to whom the investor entrusts his money or property, there are many other elements that can not only deprive the investor of the expected return on his money, but even leave him with nothing more substantial to represent his original investment than a claim against someone for something. Hope, to be sure, is never lacking to the investor, and undoubtedly many have their hopes realized and derive profit from their investments. But, because of the risks involved, even the simplest of investments requires a certain amount of business experience and acumen and, if the investment is to extend over any length of time, a knowledge of economic conditions and trends is not a disadvantage. In view of this it is only a very obvious remark to state that the present canon represents an effort on the part of the Church authorities to safeguard as far as possible the property of the Church from the risks and dangers of investment by adding to the care and diligence of the religious administrator the experience and prudent judgment of the local ordinary.

When considering the act of investing property a question arises as to whether it is an act of ordinary or extraordinary administration. In regard to this it should be noted:

1. The Code supposes that the constitutions have norms for investments, therefore that they determine which administrator has the *ordinary right* to make the investment.[1]

2. The consent required in *certain* cases is not an enabling act empowering the administrator to make an investment. No-

---

[1] Canon 533 § 1.

where does the Code forbid administrators to make investments. Rather, it prescribes them in certain cases and rightly so because investments are administrative acts which are generally necessary even though not of frequent occurrence.[2]

3. The consent of the local ordinary is not given to invest, but to invest in this or that manner. He does not relax a law forbidding investments, nor grant the faculty to invest; but merely passes judgment on the safety, utility, propriety, etc., of the particular investment contemplated by the religious administrator. It is evident therefore, that the consent of the local ordinary is required for the licitness, but not for the validity, of the act, and that an investment is an act of ordinary administration for the religious administrator. The particular administrator who enjoys this power is usually determined by the constitutions, but at times also by the Code.[3]

2. KINDS OF INVESTMENT.

Canon 533 does not stipulate the kind of investment that must be made. In general, the choice is limited either to an investment in immovable property, e. g., the purchase of lands and buildings, or in safe and fruitful movable property, e. g., the purchase of stocks, bonds, mortgages, etc. Formerly investments in immovable goods were preferred and not unfrequently prescribed. Now, on account of the danger of confiscation and on account of the difficulties of administering immovable property, investments in certain kinds of movable property are preferred and sometimes prescribed.[4] Nevertheless, if the particular law of the religious institute determines the kind of investment to be made, the administrator must follow that law.[5]

---

[2] Cf. canons 549; 1523,4°; 1531.

[3] Cf. canon 549; Vromant, *De Bonis Eccl. Temp.*, n. 230; Wernz-Vidal, *Jus Canonicum,* III, 173. Larraona, "Commentarium Codicis," *CpR,* XII (1931), 438, 439, holds that the act is extraordinary, but that the consent is only for the licitness of the act.

[4] Cf. canon 549; Larraona, *op. cit.*, p. 436, note 502.

[5] Cf. canon 533 § 1.

If the previous permission of the local ordinary is required for the investment, the choice of the investment, though it may not be dictated by him, must be satisfactory to him, since this is one of the reasons why the legislator requires the administrator to obtain the ordinary's consent.

The question may be asked whether a *deposit* of money is to be considered as an investment requiring the previous consent of the local ordinary in the cases expressed in the law.

Many authors deny this on the grounds that the one who deposits money in a bank can easily repossess himself of the money and therefore juridically it is not an investment.[6]

It seems possible in discussing this question to be misled by the terms used. Practically all bank accounts are called deposits. If the deposit is made as administrative routine for temporarily securing a sum of money, or for greater facility in paying bills and making purchases, etc., it is undoubtedly not an investment and no permission of the local ordinary is required. But if for greater security an investor chooses to place his money in a quasi-permanent way at interest in a bank, there is every reason for considering this a juridical investment. And even though this kind of investment is comparatively secure, the plan of the investment should be submitted to the approval of the local ordinary that he may be able to judge of its utility or fruitfulness. The facility with which the money may be withdrawn should not enter into the question. There are few investments that cannot be sold and turned into cash in a relatively short time. Moreover, even deposits are not without their element of risk, since the banking laws oblige the banks (even savings banks) to keep only a percentage of deposits in reserve. The rest is invested by the bank, and the interest paid to the depositor is a share of the profits made on the investment. The answer to the question seems to revolve around the nature of the deposit. If

[6] Larraona, "Commentarium Codicis," *CpR*, XII (1931), 437; Cocchi, *Commentarium*, IV, 96; Vermeersch-Creusen, *Epitome*, I, n. 602; Augustine, *A Commentary*, III, 181; Pruemmer, *Manuale J.C.*, q. 194.

the deposit is made merely for convenience or security, no permission is required; if with the intention of making one's resources productive, it is an investment and permission is required in the cases expressed by law.

3. NORMS FOR INVESTMENTS.

In regard to the norms for the investment of property the Code refers the religious administrator to the constitutions of his institute. Particular law decides which administrator has the right to make investments, the kind of investment, the formalities to be observed, and so forth. This constitutes the general norm for all investments and for all administrators. In addition to this general norm to be observed by all, canon 533 prescribes that in special cases, to be mentioned later, certain administrators are required to obtain the previous consent of the local ordinary for investments. When the consent of the local ordinary is required it should be obtained prior to the act of investment. It is sufficient that it be given orally. It may be given for each particular case, or it may be given in a general way, e. g., for certain kinds of investments, or on condition that the investment be approved by an investment counsel or person of experience, or that other formalities be observed.[7]

A. Investments by Nuns and by Sisters of Diocesan Religious Institutes

Canon 533 § 1. "*Pro pecuniae quoque collocatione servetur praescriptum can.* 532 § 1; *sed praevium consensum Ordinarii loci obtinere tenentur:*

1°. *Antista monialium et religionis iuris dioecesani pro cuiusvis pecuniae collocatione; imo, si monialium monasterium sit Superiori regulari subiectum, ipsius quoque consensus est necessarius;*"

[7] Cf. Oesterle, *Praelectiones I.C.*, I, 277; Pruemmer, *Manuale I.C.*, q. 194; Larraona, "Commentarium Codicis," *CpR*, XII (1931), 439.

1. The parties concerned in this prescript are nuns and female diocesan religious. By nuns are to be understood those mentioned in canon 488,7°, i. e., female religious who have pronounced solemn vows or whose vows are solemn *ex instituto,* but by apostolic prescript are simple in certain localities.[8] Male religious, even if of diocesan right, are not included under this law.

2. The one obligated to obtain the consent of the local ordinary and of the regular superior, when this is necessary, is the superioress of the moral person making the investment. This may be done either personally or by delegate or agent, i. e., by the religious econome.

The question has been raised whether this prescript extends to all superioresses of nuns and diocesan religious or merely to the local superioress.[9] The opinion which applies it only to the local superioress has the following difficulties to overcome:

a) It places fewer restrictions on the general and provincial administrations of diocesan institutes than it does on that of pontifical institutes. The former would not be obliged to account to any external superior, whereas the latter are obliged to make a quinquennial report to the Holy See.[10]

b) Diocesan religious, not merely in regard to their houses, but as religious, are subject to the local ordinary. What the Holy See is towards pontifical institutes, the local ordinary is towards diocesan institutes and to a great extent towards nuns, especially when not subject to a regular superior.[11]

c) To limit this obligation to local superioresses would seem to frustrate what may well be considered the very purpose of the

[8] Most authors merely state that 'nuns' are bound by this prescript. Larraona explains the term in accordance with canon 488,7°. Cf *op. cit.,* p. 440.

[9] Cf. Larraona, *op. cit.,* p. 441.

[10] Canon 510.

[11] Cf. canons 501 § 1; 618 § 1; and especially Leo XIII, const. *"Conditae a Christo,"* Dec. 8, 1900, pars. I—*Fontes,* n. 644.

law, viz., to place the vigilance of an external authority over the administration of diocesan institutes which otherwise would be without this safeguard.

d) Investments made by local administrators are few in comparison with those made by the provincial or general administrator. Moreover, some constitutions may not give to the local administrator the right to make investments.

These reasons, when considered in the light of the text of the canon which is general, indicate that the general and provincial superioresses of diocesan congregations need the consent of the local ordinary for all investments.

3. The consent for investments must be obtained by those concerned for each and every investment and change of investment. The Code makes no exceptions as to amounts.

4. The one who must give the consent is the local ordinary for diocesan congregations of women; for nuns, both the local ordinary and the regular superior, provided that the nuns are subject to a regular superior.

Besides these permissions it is also necessary to obtain the consent of those mentioned in the constitution, such as the chapter or the council, and the higher superiors.

B. Investment of Dowries

"... *praevium consensum Ordinarii loci obtinere tenentur*:

2°. *Antistita in Congregatione religiosa iuris pontificii, si pecunia dotem professarum constituat, ad normam can.* 549;"—Canon 533.

By the dowry is meant the money or property which a postulant on entering a religious institute brings with her for her support. In monasteries of nuns the postulant must have the dowry determined by the constitutions or by legitimate custom.[12]

[12] Canon 547 § 1.

These constitutions can only determine the quantity of the dowry, not the necessity of it, since this arises from a prescript of law.[13] The right to condone this dowry in whole or in part for nuns and for all religious of pontifical right can be obtained only from the Holy See.[14]

In religious institutes of simple vows the constitutions determine both the necessity and the quantity of the dowry.[15] If the institute is of diocesan right, the constitutions in regard to this can be relaxed by the local ordinary, or with his permission.[16]

The law for dowries, as mentioned in canon 533 § 1,2°, concerns only female religious of congregations of pontifical right, but the obligation contained therein already rests on the superioress of nuns and of diocesan institutes in virtue of the preceding number 1° of canon 533.

The superioress obligated is the one who in the constitutions is empowered to invest the dowries of professed religious. Usually this will be the provincial superioress. The "*Normae*" of 1901 required that the dowry be secured to the institute, not to the house. Logically then, the higher superioresses should administer it.[17] The Code implies the same by requiring that the administration be conducted at the habitual residence of the general or provincial superioress.[18]

After the religious has made her first profession, the superioress empowered by the constitutions to invest the dowry must invest it in safe, legal, and fruitful securities. It is not advisable, as a rule, to invest this money in immovable property for

---

[13] The *Normae* (n. 91) suppose that lay sisters will also have a dowry, but less than that required of the choir sisters.

[14] Canon 547 § 4.

[15] Canon 547 § 3.

[16] Canon 547 § 4.

[17] *Normae secundum quas S.C.Ep. et Reg. procedere solet in approbandis novis institutis votorum simplicium,* Romae, 1901, n. 93.

[18] Cf. canon 550 § 1. Larraona admits the opinion that a local superioress may invest and administer the dowries. Cf. *op cit.*, XII (1931), 442.

the reason that it may have to be returned to the religious, and this might be difficult if it has been invested in land or buildings.

Before making the investment the superioress must obtain the vote of her consultors. It is not clear from the Code that their consent is necessary for the validity of the act. It suffices, then, if she hear their opinion in the matter.[19] She must also for the licitness of her act obtain the previous permission of the local ordinary, and, if the nuns are subject to a regular superior, his permission must be added to the others.[20]

It is absolutely forbidden to the religious administrator to use the capital of the dowry in any way whatever before the death of the religious. Not even the construction of a religious house nor the extinction of a debt will justify such use. Permission for this can be obtained from the Holy See alone, and then only for the most grave reasons.[21]

The administration of the dowry must be conducted prudently and in its entirety at the habitual residence of the general or provincial superioress.[22]

The local ordinary of the place where the dowries are administered has a special obligation to see that the principal of the dowry is conserved.[23] For this end the religious administrator should have a book in which are noted the dowries received, the manner of their investment, etc.[24] This book or any other documents pertaining to the dowries and their administration are subject to examination by the local ordinary whenever he may deem it necessary. Moreover, he must require an account of the entire administration of the dowries at least once a year in the

---

[19] Canon 105,1°, Vromant, *De Bonis Eccl. Temp.*, n. 255.

[20] Canon 549.

[21] Canon 549; S.C. de Rel., instr. *"Inter ea,"* July 30, 1909, n. XII—*AAS*, I (1909), 698.

[22] Canon 550 § 1; cf. above, p. 98.

[23] Canon 550 § 2.

[24] Choupin, *Nature et Obligations de l'ètat religieux*, p. 272.

case of nuns,[25] and for other religious at least every five years at the time of the visitation.[26]

If a religious leave the religious institute for any reason whatever, the dowry which she offered on entering must be restored to her in its entirety. It is unimportant whether the vows of the religious be solemn or simple. However, the income, interest, or dividends which had been earned by the invested principal of the dowry up to the moment when the religious departed from the institute is retained by the institute as compensation for the support of the religious.

If the value of the invested dowry has decreased through no fault of the administrator, only the value which it has at the moment of the departure of the religious need be returned to her. If this decrease in value has taken place along with other investments, then a proportionate sum should be returned to the religious. However, if at the time of accepting the dowry it was agreed to return a definite sum in case of the departure of the religious, the sum agreed upon must be returned.[27]

If the religious has been accepted into the religious institute without any or with a very small dowry and has not sufficient property to provide for herself, the institute, if she leaves, must in charity furnish her with what is adequate to return safely and conveniently to her home, and must also provide for her honest support for a period of time to be determined by mutual agreement between the institute and the ex-religious, or by the local ordinary.[28] The manner in which this obligation has been fulfilled must be stated in the quinquennial report of pontifical institutes to the Holy See.[29]

---

[25] Canon 535 § 1,1°.

[26] Canons 512; 535 § 2; 550 § 2.

[27] Vromant, *De Bonis Eccl. Temp.*, n. 256; Creusen, *Het Kloosterleven*, n. 152.

[28] Canon 643 § 2; S.C. de Rel., 2 March 1924—*AAS*, XVI (1924), 165.

[29] S.C. de Rel., instr. March 25, 1922—*AAS*, XV (1923), 459.

If in virtue of an apostolic indult a religious transfers to another religious institute, her dowry continues to be administered by the former institute, until she makes her profession in the new institute. However, during her novitiate the income of the dowry must be handed over to the new institute, and upon her profession in the new institute, the dowry itself.[30]

Canon 551 § 2, in stating this law, says that the prescript of Canon 570 § 1 continues to be in force. This canon forbids a religious institute to demand anything of a novice or postulant for the expenses of the novitiate or postulancy unless, as in the case of food and the religious habit, the constitutions permit it or an express agreement has been made. Vromant, following Vermeersch and Creusen, states that if the institute does not demand anything during the time of the novitiate or postulancy, the fruits of the dowry may be kept by the former institute during the time preceding the profession of the religious in the new institute.[31] Bastien on the other hand thinks that the income of the dowry must always be transferred to the new institute.[32] This opinion seems to correspond more closely to the wording of the Code which states clearly that during the novitiate the income of the dowry is due to the institute to which the religious has transferred. The clause referring to canon 570 § 1 seems to indicate that notwithstanding this arrangement, the new institute has a right to receive compensation for food and habit from the religious, if this is permitted by the constitutions or has been expressly agreed upon. The institute from which the religious has departed seems to have no grounds in law or in fact on which it may claim the income of the dowry once the religious has left; except perhaps, on the score of administrative expenses which would usually be too slight to receive notice. The arrangement mentioned above, however, might prove bur-

[30] Canon 551 § 2.

[31] Vromant, *De Bonis Eccl. Temp.*, n. 256; Vermeersch-Creusen, *Epit.*, I, n. 652; Creusen, *Religieux et Religieuses*, n. 153.

[32] *Dir. Can.*, n. 105.

densome to the religious making the transfer. It would seem equitable if the competent superior would accept the income from the dowry as payment or part payment of anything which might be due to the institute during the time of the novitiate.

If a professed religious transfers from one monastery to another of the same order, the dowry which she brought with her to the monastery must go with her to the monastery to which she transfers.[33]

C. Investment of Donations Given for Local Purposes

> " . . . *praevium consensum Ordinarii loci obtinere tenentur*:
>
> 3°. *Superior vel Antistita domus Congregationis religiosae, si qui fundi domui tributi legative sint ad Dei cultum beneficentiamve eo ipso loco impendendam;*"—Canon 533.

Three principal questions engage the attention of canonists in regard to the meaning of this prescript: 1. The nature of the property involved; 2. The class of religious who are bound by it, i. e., the extent of the prescript; 3. The superior who is bound by it; whether all superiors are bound by this prescript, or merely local superiors?

I. The Nature of the Property Involved

1. The word used by the Code to describe the property involved in this prescript is the word '*fundus.*' The ordinary meaning of *fundus* gives the idea of landed possessions. It is best expressed in English by the term 'real-estate' or 'real property.' This is also the meaning it had in Roman Law.[34] Undoubtedly,

---

[33] Canon 551 § 2.

[34] "Fundi appellatione omne aedificium et omnis ager continetur." "Ager cum aedificio fundus dicitur."—D. (50, 16) 211. "Fundus est omne, quid-

however, the Code refers to more than real-estate. The whole of canon 533 is concerned with the investment of money. Other property is considered, but only in so far as it has been or will be converted into money, or is in a form capable of being invested. In regard, however, to the account of administration, the prescript of canon 535 § 3,2° extends to all kinds of property.

2. The property in question has been acquired by the religious house by *donation*. This donation may have been received either in the form *inter vivos* or *mortis causa,* as is clear from the words *"tributi legative"* which appear in the text.[35] It seems necessary to emphasize the fact that this prescript treats only of donations. Whatever may be considered the *income* of the house, either regular, as salary, stole fees, etc., or exceptional, as a subsidy for the house from the bishop or higher superiors, does not come under this prescript.[36]

3. The property itself is to be conserved and only the income from it may be used. This is evident from the fact that the property is to be invested; also from the source of this canon which indicates, as a reason for the supervision of the ordinary, the desire to keep the property intact.[37] It follows from this that not every donation comes under consideration in this prescript, but only those that are to be invested and conserved.

---

quid solo tenetur."—D. (50, 16) 115. Fundus [singular]—"fortuna, possessio." Fundi [plural]—"praedia, campi, agri vel campi vel possessiones." Cf. *Thesaurus Linguae Latinae,* VI, col. 1579.

[35] It must be certain that the donation has been made to the religious as such, and not to a church or parish of which they have charge. If after examination a doubt remains about any particular donation, it is necessary to presume that the donation has been given to the church or parish of which the religious have charge, and then the consent of the local ordinary is required for its investment in accordance with canon 533 § 1,4°. Cf. can. 1536 § 1.

[36] "Singularum vero familiarum redditus a praesidibus singulis administrari oportet, pro instituti cuiusque legibus. De iis nullam Episcopus rationem potest exigere."—Leo XIII, const. *"Conditae a Christo,"* Dec. 8, 1900, pars II, n. IX—*Fontes,* n. 644.

[37] *Ibid.*

4. The income of this property is to be used for defraying the expenses of divine worship or of some charitable undertaking that is local in character.[38]

Divine Worship.—If the donation is for Masses, church services, etc., in that very place; or for the building, conservation, restoration or decoration of a church, provided the church belongs to the place or diocese. If the church belongs to the religious themselves the religious superiors are allowed to administer the donation.[39]

Charitable Projects.—Under this heading may come any spiritual or corporal work of mercy: Masses, church services, catechising, care of orphanages, hospitals, teaching school, aid to the poor, etc.

Local Benefit.—This idea is best explained by canon 1516 § 3, which speaks of charitable trusts as a benefit for the churches, inhabitants, or pious causes of a place or diocese. It seems that the prescripts of these two canons (can. 533 § 1,3° and 1516 § 3) are coextensive in regard to their object, and that the purpose of the law in each case is to remove any doubt about the right of the local ordinary to supervise the administration of property in which he has an interest because of its relation to persons or places under his jurisdiction or *tutela*.[40] For the same reason however, it seems that property given to the religious for their support, or for the upkeep of their houses and churches, novitiates, etc., is not comprehended *by this prescript*, even though the donation be used locally.[41] As to this, however, it

---

[38] ". . . ad Dei cultum beneficentiamve eo ipso loco impendendam;"—Can. 533 § 1,3°.

[39] Cf. canon 630 § 4; Signatura Apostolica, *De Manila*, 6 Apr. 1920—*AAS*, XII (1920), 257.

[40] "Ideo parochus vel ecclesiae rector facere non potest quin rationes reddat ordinario loci, cuius est iurisdictio et causae piae tutela."—Leo XIII, *"Romanos Pontifices,"* 8 May 1881, n. 24—*Fontes*, n. 582; S.C.C. *Nullius*, 27 June 1744—*Thesaurus*, XIII, 97.

[41] *"By this prescript"*—Nuns and diocesan religious would be accountable

must be *certain* that the intention of the donor is primarily to favor the religious institute, house, etc. If the principal intention is to favor a diocesan project, and only indirectly a religious house, then the local ordinary has the right of supervision even in the case of regulars conducting parishes and missions, for in this case it is presumed that the donation has been given in view of the parish or mission. An example will make this clear.—The ownership of a house and land that produced a yearly income was transferred to a community of teaching sisters. One of the reasons for the transfer of this property was that the sisters might have a place to live and a yearly income for their support. (Certainly these objects are intimately connected with the sisters, as sisters.) But the principal reason for the transfer was that the place might be benefited to the extent of having sisters who would teach in the school.—In a dispute about the ownership of this property, the Sacred Roman Rota decided that the ownership belonged to the sisters, but "ad formam can. 533 § 1,3°,4° et can. 535 § 3,2°."[42]

5. When the above circumstances are put together it is impossible to exclude from this prescript that class of donations known as *pious foundations.* In many cases all the conditions for such will be present: 1. Temporal goods; 2. Acquired by an ecclesiastical moral person; 3. With the perpetual or long time obligation; 4. To use the revenues; 5. For divine worship or a charitable project.—Now all these conditions constitute a pious foundation,[43] therefore the prescript of canon 533 § 1,3° should be considered as applicable to pious foundations. However, it is

---

to the local ordinary for the administration of such property in virtue of canon 535 § 1,1° and § 3,1°.

[42] S.R.R., 13 Aug. 1926—*S.R. Rotae Decisiones,* XVIII (1926), dec. XLIII, n. 24; Cf. Signatura Apostolica, *Manila,* 6 Apr. 1920—*AAS,* XII (1920), 257, 258; Pont. Comm., 25 July 1926—*AAS,* XVIII (1926), 393.

[43] Canon 1544.

also applicable to other donations and 'foundations' which cannot be strictly called 'pious foundations.'[44]

6. If canon 533 § 1,3° is applied to pious foundations, it will perhaps be objected that it will then be necessary to apply to these donations or legacies the laws for pious foundations as stated in canons 1544-1551, and not merely the prescripts of canons 533 § 1,3° and 535 § 3,2°. This does not seem to be necessary. The laws for pious foundations, stated in canons 1544-1551, apply to religious only when they are established in the parishes or churches of religious. When established in the houses of religious they are governed by the laws of canons 533-535. The reasons on which this opinion is based are as follows:

(1) The laws for the administration of property acquired by the institute, province, or house are found in canons 532-537. Even though supplementary laws are found elsewhere in the Code, they can always be reconciled with those found in the above canons, except if one tries to apply canons 1544-1551 to pious foundations established in the *houses* of religious. There seems to be no equivalent for these laws in canons 532-537.[45]

---

[44] It is sometimes difficult to know whether a donation is to be considered as a pious foundation or merely as a foundation (e. g., of a church, school, benefice etc.). A *foundation* for a religious house is a donation *"ad sedem et dotem"* (Cf. S.R.R., 13 Aug. 1926—*S.R. Rotae Decisiones*, XVIII [1926], dec. XLIII, n. 6), enabling the religious to carry on the work to which they have dedicated themselves by their Rule. A *Pious Foundation* to a religious house would usually require of the religious something *extra* or in addition to that which by Rule they are obliged to do, though it may be of the same nature. The obligations must be specified in the *Pious Foundation*, whereas the same obligations in a *Foundation* would be implied or innate. (Cf. S.R.R., 9 Aug. 1924—*S.R. Rotae Decisiones*, XVI [1924], dec. XXXIX, n. 2.) The long time must be specified in the *Pious Foundation;* it is not specified, but may be just as long in the *Foundation*.

[45] Cf. Larraona, "Commentarium Codicis," *CpR*, XIII (1932), 29, note 544; Fagalde, *De Privilegio Exemptionis*, pp. 37-39; Pruemmer, *Manuale I.C.*, q. 194; Nebreda, *"De Loci Ordinariorum Juribus, . . ." CpR*, VII (1926), 329.

(2) The generality of canonists admit that canon 533 § 1,3° applies to pious foundations acquired by houses of religious.[46] There is no need therefore of applying canons 1544-1550 to the *houses* of religious.

(3) The difficulty arising from attempting to reconcile these two groups of canons disappears if canons 532-537 are applied to *houses* of religious, and canons 1544-1550 to *churches* of religious.

(4) There is reason for separating the two for the fact that pious foundations established in churches will usually be concerned with Masses or church services, and over these the local ordinary has the right and duty of greater vigilance, unless they are established in churches of exempt religious. Moreover, the fact that a pious foundation has been established in a church rather than in a house of religious, will often indicate that the donor wishes that the obligations be satisfied in that church (*eo ipso loco*) and not elsewhere. Hence, even though the religious depart from the locality, the church will in all probability remain, and the obligations attached to it will continue. In view of this possibility it can be seen that the local ordinary has a concern and an interest in the obligations assumed by the church, and should, therefore, have corresponding powers. On the other hand, obligations assumed by the community go with the community wherever they go, and therefore, the power of the local ordinary over these need not be so extensive. This seems to be made clear by the canons on religious administration. Of these canons only the prescript of canon 533 § 1,3° can apply to pious foundations. Now, according to that prescript the local ordinary has the right of supervision only when the foundation has been acquired by a *house* (not a province), and then only when the obligations are to be satisfied locally (*eo ipso loco*). To argue, then, that canons 1544-1550 apply to pious foundations acquired by *houses* of religious, is to hold the view either that canon 533 does not apply to any pious foundations, or that the

---

[46] Cf. Larraona, *loc. cit.*

Legislator introduced contradictory or at least irreconcilable laws into the Code.[47]

7. In view of the above the following are the rules governing donations that come under the prescript of canon 533 § 1,3°, whether they are pious foundations or not:

a) If acquired by nuns or diocesan religious, the entire administration including the investment, is subject to the supervision of the local ordinary in virtue of canons 533 § 1,1° and 535 § 1,1° and §3,1°.

b) If acquired by houses of non-exempt pontifical institutes for the support of divine worship or a pious cause in the place or diocese where the house is located, the local ordinary must give permission for its investment and receive an account of its administration in virtue of canons 533 § 1,3° and 535 § 3,2°.

c) If acquired by exempt religious, except nuns, the administration is entirely subject to the major superiors, unless it is acquired in view of a parish or mission.[48]

8. *Eo ipso loco.*—The more common opinion is that these words do not refer merely to the district or town where the house is located but to the whole diocese.[49] It would be strange if the

[47] The source of the trouble seems to be the prevalent view that the religious house and church constitute one moral person, so that if the legislator says *house* in canon 533, he means also *church;* if he says *church* in canon 1550, he means also *house.* There is much to sustain the view on practical grounds. However, in fact and in theory there is a difference between the two, and the Code brings out the difference in several places (cf. canons 99, 1182 § 3, 1495 § 2). May it not be possible that canon 1550 is another instance where the legislator makes use of the distinction between church and house? De Luca, who seems to be the authority for the view that church and house are one moral person, does not go beyond the statement that "neque inter claustra, seu recinctum et ecclesiam ibi adnexam *et incorporatam* adesse videtur *notabilis* differentia"—*De Parochis,* disc. XXIII, n. 14.

[48] Cf. below, II.

[49] Brandys, *Kirchliches Rechtsbuch,* p. 189; De Meester, *Jus Can. Comp.,* II, n. 980; Schaefer, *De Religiosis,* p. 331; Vermeersch-Creusen, *Epitome,*

local ordinary had the right to supervise the administration of property in one section of his diocese and not in another. The fact that should be ascertained is: has the local ordinary a right to supervise the administration of *this property?* If he has he may exercise that right anywhere in his diocese. However, even if this restricted interpretation could be proved, it could not be made use of by nuns or diocesan religious who are under the supervision of the local ordinary in virtue of other prescripts.[50]

II. *The Religious Who Are Bound By This Prescript*

The wording of this prescript makes it certain that all non-exempt religious are bound by it, and that regulars, with the exception of nuns, are not bound by it.[51] The doubt is limited to the application of this prescript to exempt clerical congregations.[52]

I, n. 606; Aliter Larraona, "Commentarium Codicis," *CpR*, XIII (1932), 34; Wernz-Vidal, *Jus Canonicum*, III, 174.

[50] Canons 533 § 1,1°; 535 § 3,1°.

[51] Nuns are bound to this prescript in virtue of the more general prescript already treated under number one of this canon. Cf. pp. 96 ff.

[52] The sides taken by the various canonists are:

1. Against applying this prescript to religious of exempt clerical institutes are: Vermeersch-Creusen, *Epitome*, I, n. 606; Raus, *Inst. Can.*, p. 209; Oesterle, *Prael. I. C.*, I, 277; De Meester, *Jus Can. Comp.* II, n. 980; Vromant, *De Bonis Eccl. Temp.*, nn. 234, 354; Schoensteiner, *Grundriss des Ordensrechts*, p. 228; Jansen, *Ordensrecht*, p. 109; Bastien, *Dir. Can.* n. 316; Vleider, *Leitfaden zum Studium des k. Rechtsbuches*, I, 612; Nebreda, "De Loci Ordinariorum Juribus, . . ." *CpR*, VII (1926), 321; Berutti, *Inst. I.C.*, III, 117.

2. In favor of applying this prescript to exempt clerical religious are: Augustine, *A Commentary*, III, 181; Biederlack-Fuerich, *De Religiosis*, p. 97; Bouuaert-Simenon, *Manuale I.C.*, p. 632; Chelodi, *Ius de Personis*, n. 260; Schaefer, *De Religiosis*, p. 238; Pejska, *Jus Can. Rel.*, p. 64; Pruemmer, *Manuale I.C.*, q. 194; Fanfani, *De Jure Rel.*, n. 155; Blat, *Commentarium*, II, 581; Larraona, "Commentarium Codicis," *CpR*, XIII (1932), 25; Wernz-Vidal, *Jus Can.*, III, 176.

3. Seemingly doubtful are: a Coronata, *Inst. I.C.*, p. 674; Cocchi, *Commentarium*, IV, 96.

There is no doubt that the words "*congregationis religiosae*" are general enough to include all religious of simple vows, and therefore even those exempt. However, in view of canon 615, which excludes exempt religious from subjection to the local ordinary except in the cases expressed in the law,[53] and in view of the practice of the legislator to mention exempt religious expressly when he wishes them included in the law,[54] one may reasonably doubt whether it is the intention of the legislator to include exempt religious under this prescript.

Considering for a moment the canons on pious foundations (1544-1551), it is seen that exempt religious are certainly not subject to the jurisdiction of the local ordinary in regard to pious foundations established in their churches.[55] But it has been shown that pious foundations are included under the prescript of canon 533 § 1,3°.[56] The result is, then, two laws applying to the same matter under slightly different circumstances. In one case the foundation is established in the house of the religious; in the other case, in the church of the religious. The extent of one is certain. A reasonable doubt can be raised regarding the extent of the other. Under the circumstances there should be no hesitation in determining the extent of the doubtful canon 533 by the clear canon 1550, and in this way excluding exempt religious from the prescript contained in canon 533 § 1,3°. If this is valid in regard to pious foundations, *a fortiori* in regard

[53] Regulars are exempt by law, some other religious institutes by privilege. The extent of the privilege must be judged from the document by which it was granted. That the Passionists and Redemptorists "gaudent omnimoda exemptione ab Episcopali iurisdictione, visitatione et correctione, exceptis casibus iure excipiendis," is evidenced by a discussion of the question and a decree of the S.C.EE. et RR., 16 Sept. 1864. Cf. *ASS*, I (1865-66), 91-99.

[54] Cf. canons 296 § 1; 297; 512; 612; 616; 617; 804 § 3; 831,3°; 1261 § 2; 1274 § 1; 1293; 1303 § 3; 1334; 1336; 1345; 1382.

[55] Canon 1550.

[56] Above p. 105.

to other donations, excepting always those granted in view of the parish or mission.[57]

The only serious objection to this opinion has been raised by Father Larraona, who claims that in the early drafts of the Code the words '*non exemptae*' were found in this prescript, which read: "*Superior vel Antistita domus Congregationis religiosae non exemptae. . . .*" These words, he claims, were stricken out of the promulgated edition to indicate the legislator's intention to include *all* religious of simple vows, even those exempt. If the deduction is correct, discussion of this matter ends here. Still it cannot be denied that this suggested purpose of the legislator would have been better served by changing the words from '*non exemptae*' to '*etiam exemptae.*' This is the usual style of the legislator, and in accord with the law; and it would have removed all doubt.

In holding that this prescript does not apply to exempt clerical religious, it is only intended to extend the principle to property acquired by the religious house. If acquired by a religious parish (canon 1425), or by a parish entrusted to religious (can. 456), or by a religious house but in view of a parish or mission, the ordinary of the place has the right of supervision allowed by canons 533 § 1,3°,4° and 535 § 3,2°.[58]

III. *The Superiors Bound By This Prescript*

The wording of the Code in this prescript clearly refers to local superiors (*Superior vel antistita domus*). Provincial, vice-provincial, and general superiors, therefore, have no obligation from this prescript to obtain the previous permission of the local ordinaries. However, since the type of investment considered in this prescript is included in the more general prescript of canon

[57] Cf. the authors cited above in favor of this view.

[58] Cf. Pont. Comm. 25 July 1926—*AAS*, XVIII (1926), 393; Signatura Apostolica, *Manila*, 6 April 1920—*AAS*, XII (1920), 257, 258; S.R.R., 13 Aug. 1926—*S.R. Rotae Decisiones*, XVIII (1926), dec. XLIII, n. 24.

533 § 1,1°, higher superiors of nuns and diocesan religious would be bound to obtain the previous permission of the local ordinary.[59] Thus, in effect, only the higher superiors of pontifical institutes are exempt from this prescript.[60]

Summary

To summarize the foregoing commentary on canon 533 § 1,3°, it may be stated:

1. If property or money has been donated or willed to a religious house of non-exempt religious or of nuns with the obligation of using the money or the income therefrom in defraying the expenses of divine worship or of a religious or charitable project within the limits of and for the benefit of the diocese where the money was donated or willed, the superior or superioress of the house (or whoever is in charge of the administration of this fund) must obtain the previous permission of the local ordinary before investing it or changing the investment.

2. If the property or money has been donated or willed to the house without any obligations or with obligations that can be satisfied in the manner and place determined by the religious themselves, religious of pontifical institutes are not subject to the local ordinary regarding its investment, unless they be nuns. Nuns and diocesan religious are subject to the local ordinary in virtue of canon 533 § 1,1°.

---

[59] Cf. above, pp. 96 ff.

[60] The exemption of the higher superiors seems to be brought out clearly in the case *De Manila* of the Signatura Apostolica (6 Apr. 1920—*AAS*, XII [1920], 252-259). Legacies with the obligation of Masses were left under identical conditions and by the same person to a province of regulars and also to a house of the same regulars. When the parish was taken from the regulars and entrusted to a secular priest, he claimed the right to administer both legacies. The S. R. Rota issued two decisions against the petitioner. He thereupon had recourse to the Signatura Apostolica and was granted a *restitutio in integrum*, but only in regard to the legacy left to the house. The reason for this was that the nature of the legacy left to the *house* had not been sufficiently examined in view of canon 533 §

D. Investment of Donations to a Parish or Mission

"... *sed praevium consensum Ordinarii loci obtinere tenentur:*

4°. *Religiosus quilibet, etsi Ordinis regularis alumnus, si pecunia data sit paroeciae vel missioni, aut religiosis intuitu paroeciae vel missionis.*"—Canon 533.

This prescript extends to all religious, whether regulars or not, and whether superior or subjects.

It includes all donations and offerings made in view of a parish or mission. Therefore, not only those given directly for the parish or mission, but even those made to the religious house or church or to the religious themselves, if the donor intends that they be used for the purposes of the parish or mission.

The donation may be of any kind. The canon speaks of money, but this refers to the form the donation will take for investment. When given it may be either movable or immovable property. It may be given in any way, i. e., by donation, legacy, or manual gift.

The parish which is intended as the beneficiary of this gift may be either a secular parish or a religious parish (canon 1425). If a parish has been united *pleno iure* to a religious house and in this way has become a religious benefice, the religious are not entitled to the entire income of that parish, but only to the beneficial fruits.[61]

1,3°,4°, since it might have been given with obligations to be satisfied *eo ipso loco;* or given to the religious house, but *intuitu paroeciae vel missionis.* Now since the legacy given to the province was given under the same conditions as that given to the house, this decision seems to indicate that the prescripts of canon 533 § 1,3°,4° regard only houses and local superiors.

[61] This states a general rule. No consideration is given here to particular agreements between religious and local ordinaries. As to the rule, cf. Leo XIII, const. "*Romanos Pontifices,*" 8 maii 1881, n. 24—*Fontes*, n. 582. *Concilii Plenarii Baltimorensis Tertii Acta et Decreta,* n. 90; *Pont. Comm.*, 25 July 1926—*AAS,* XVIII (1926), 393.

By a mission is generally understood the whole territory of a vicariate or prefecture apostolic, and not merely a limited district of such, or a quasi-parish.[62] In this sense the word mission connotes some definite territory and not missions in general as the word is popularly used. If missionaries receive donations for the mission entrusted to them, the investment and administration of these donations are subject to the vicar or prefect apostolic of the mission designated, or of the mission to which the donation is sent, if none has been designated.[63]

At times it may be difficult to determine when the donation has been given to the religious for themselves and when for the parish or mission. It is of prime importance, therefore, in regard to formal donations and gifts, that as far as possible and as soon as possible the intention of the donor in regard to the purpose of the gift and the recipient of the gift should be made manifest by a document capable of supplying proof. It is also important that religious in charge of parishes or missions make an inventory of the property that belongs to them as religious and that which belongs to the parish or mission.[64] This procedure is of course not possible in regard to most free-will offerings made in connection with the church or parish. The following rules may be an aid in determining the nature of these offerings.

1. If the donor intends to bestow a benefit on the religious themselves, the gift is acquired by the religious and administered by them. In this case the only religious required to obtain permission for investing these offerings will be nuns and female diocesan religious in virtue of canon 533 § 1,1°.

2. If the donor intends to bestow a benefit on the work of the religious, a further distinction is necessary to determine whether

---

[62] S.C. de Prop. Fide, ep. Easter 1922—*AAS*, XIV (1922), 287-302; Leo XIII, const. *"Romanos Pontifices," loc. cit.*, n. 14.

[63] S.C. de Prop. Fide, instr. 8 Dec. 1929—*AAS*, XXII (1930), 111; S.C. de Prop. Fide, 28 July 1932—Bouscaren, *Canon Law Digest*, p. 191.

[64] S.C. de Prop. Fide, 10 May 1868—*Fontes*, n. 582.

the work is under the control of the religious superior or under that of a local ordinary.

In the first case only nuns and female diocesan religious will have to obtain the permission of the local ordinary in virtue of the canon mentioned above. In the second case all religious, whether exempt or not, will have to give an account and obtain the consent of the local ordinary for investing such offerings. The reason for both of these regulations is stated as follows by Pope Leo XIII:

> Every offering given to a pastor or to a rector of a church in view of any pious cause, is acquired by the pious cause. Hence the recipient of the offering holds the place of an administrator, whose duty it is to administer the offering according to the mind and will of the donor. But since it is also the duty of an administrator to keep an account of his administration, and render it to the one whose business is transacted, it follows that the pastor or rector cannot do otherwise than give an account of his administration to the local ordinary to whose jurisdiction and protection the pious cause belongs.[65]

For the United States the decrees of the Council of Baltimore will be a further help in determining the destination of certain free will offerings. In 1885, at the request of the Third Plenary Council of Baltimore, the Constitution *"Romanos Pontifices"* was extended by Pope Leo XIII to the Church of the United States.[66] Borrowing the words of this papal constitution the Council of Baltimore decreed as follows:

1. Missionaries of regular orders are not bound to render to the Bishop an account of the property pertaining to them as regulars.

---

[65] Const. *"Romanos Pontifices,"* 8 May 1881, n. 24—*Fontes,* n. 582.

[66] S.C.P.F., decretum, 25 Sept. 1885—*Concilii Plenarii Baltimorensis Tertii Acta et Decreta,* Murphy: Baltimore, 1886, p. cv.

2. The Bishops have a right to demand an account of property given to the mission or to the regulars in view of the mission, in the same way that they may demand this account of secular pastors.

3. The method of determining what has been offered in view of the missions is that defined by the Second Provincial Council of Westminster.[67]

In the Second Provincial Council of Westminster the following offerings are considered as made to the parish or mission, and an account of them had to be made to the bishop. It did not matter whether the pastor was a religious of simple or solemn vows, or whether the church was the property of the religious or of the diocese. 1. Pew rent; 2. Offertory collections;[68] 3. Seat collections; 4. Collections taken up at special sermons; 5. House to house collections.[69]

4. CHANGE OF INVESTMENT.

> § 2. "*Haec item servanda sunt pro qualibet collocationis mutatione.*"—Canon 533.

Since the ordinary, in giving his consent to any particular investment, forms a judgment only about the security or utility of that particular investment, it follows that the withdrawal of all or part of the funds from the original investment to reinvest them in a different manner or with a different company amounts

---

[67] *Ibid.*, n. 90; cf. also, Leo XIII, const., *"Romanos Pontifices,"* 8 May 1881, n. 26—*Fontes*, n. 582.

[68] The III Plenary C. of Balt. considered all collections taken up in the church to be revenues of the church unless the bishop had determined otherwise—cf. n. 273.

[69] *Ibid.*, appendix, p. 231. According to Barrett, the decrees of Baltimore on this matter contain nothing contrary to the Code, so nothing of it is set aside by the Code.—Cf. *A Comparative Study of the Councils of Baltimore and the Code of Canon Law*, The Cath. Univ. of Am., Canon Law Studies, n. 83; Wash., D. C., 1932, p. 106.

in reality to a new investment. The law therefore prescribes that the same permissions are necessary for the change of an investment as for the original investment. Only when the original investment, having been withdrawn, is reinvested under the same conditions as the first investment, may it be presumed that the consent of the local ordinary continues and that no new consent is required. Thus if government bonds are redeemed at maturity, the money realized can be reinvested in the same kind of bonds without a new permission of the local ordinary.[70]

---

[70] Schaefer, *De Religiosis*, n. 198; Leitner, *Handbuch des Ordensrechtes*, p. 374; Schoensteiner, *Grundiss des Ordensrechtes*, p. 299.

CHAPTER IV

ALIENATIONS—DEBTS—OBLIGATIONS

CANON 534

§ 1. "*Firmo praescripto can.* 1531, *si agatur de alienandis rebus pretiosis aliisve bonis quorum valor superet summam triginta millium francorum seu libellarum, vel de contrahendis debitis et obligationibus ultra indicatam summam, contractus vi caret, nisi beneplacitum apostolicum antecesserit; secus, requiritur et sufficit licentia, in scriptis data, Superioris ad normam constitutionum cum consensu sui Capituli seu Consilii per secreta suffragia manifestato; sed si agatur de monialibus aut sororibus iuris dioecesani, accedat necesse est consensus, in scriptis praestitus, Ordinarii loci, necnon Superioris regularis, si monialium monasterium eidem subiectum sit.*"

The scope of canon 534 is to determine the conditions under which ecclesiastical property belonging to religious may be alienated or obligated. It cannot be denied that the Church is rigorous and exacting in this matter. But such an attitude is justified for the reason that the real owner of the property to be alienated or obligated is not the one who performs the juridical act, but the ecclesiastical moral person by whom the property has been acquired.[1]

In law moral persons are considered as minors[2] and are necessarily represented by official administrators. To procure the best interests of the moral person and to assist the administra-

[1] Canon 1499 § 2.

[2] Canon 100 § 3.

tors in their grave and difficult task the Church, tutored by a long and varied experience, lays down in this canon the rules and regulations by which the religious administrator must be guided in alienating and obligating the property of the religious moral person.

In this treatise only the property acquired by religious moral persons comes under consideration. If religious are administrators of ecclesiastical property that is not religious property, it is clear that they are bound by the general Church Law on alienation and contracts and subject to the ecclesiastical superior having jurisdiction over the property in question, unless stated otherwise in a particular agreement.[3] When the property in question is strictly religious property, canon 534 is supplementary to the general norms for the alienation of church property, and religious superiors and administrators *"have an obligation in conscience* of fully carrying out the prescriptions of canon 534 § 1 of the Code of Canon Law. And this obligation *extends to all religious* including regulars and other exempt religious."[4]

1. MEANING OF ALIENATION.

In the strict sense alienation is that act by which the direct ownership of religious property is transferred to another person whether physical or moral. The transfer may be made on an onerous or gratuitous title; and may take place by exchange, loan, sale, gift or legacy.[5]

---

[3] Cf. canons 1529-1551.

[4] Cf. Letter of the Apostolic Delegate to Religious Superiors, Wash., D. C., Nov. 13, 1936.—*Note*: This letter, which will be referred to throughout this chapter, was communicated to religious superiors in the United States by His Excellency, the Most Rev. A. G. Cicognani, Apostolic Delegate to the United States, on the authorization of the Sacred Congregation of Religious.

[5] Wernz, *Jus Decr.*, III, 177; Waffelaert, *De Justitia*, n. 524; Vromant, *op. cit.*, n. 279; Larraona, *op. cit.*, p. 188; Cleary, *Canonical Limitations on*

In a wide sense, and as used in the Code of Canon Law, alienation includes not only the transfer of ownership as above, but also any act by which an administrator, without giving up the direct ownership, transmits or remits to another an incorporeal right (*jus in re*) in such a way that the ownership of religious property is limited or made less secure, as by a mortgage, or lease.[6]

The equivalent of alienation in the sense of canon 534 are all contractual debts and obligations by which the financial condition of the religious moral person is rendered less secure, even though there be no transfer of property or of property rights. In regard to this it is not necessary that the transaction be unprofitable. If the religious moral person is thereafter burdened with a debt or obligation, even though a profit was realized from the transaction, the transaction is the equivalent of alienation.[7]

2. OBJECT OF ALIENATION.

Under this heading will be considered (*a*) the property with which this canon is concerned; (*b*) the acts with which it is concerned; (*c*) the acts with which it is not concerned.

A. The Property

1. In this place only religious ecclesiastical property is being considered, i. e., such as has been acquired by an ecclesiastical moral person that is at the same time religious, as a religious institute, province, vice-province, or house. The private property, of which religious of simple vows retain the ownership according to canon 580 § 1, is not subject to the prescriptions of canon 534, because it is not religious property. But all religious

---

the Alienation of Church Property, Cath. Univ. of Am., Canon Law Studies, n. 100, Wash., D. C., 1936, p. 94.

[6] Pejska, *Jus Can. Rel.*, p. 70; Larraona, *loc. cit.*

[7] Santi-Leitner, lib. III, tit. 23, *de solicitationibus;* Ojetti, *Synopsis*, n. 593; Larraona, *op. cit.*, p. 189; Vromant, *op. cit.*, nn. 296, 307.

ecclesiastical property is subject to this canon even though the religious owner has not obtained or cannot obtain civil incorporation, or even when for any reason whatever the civil ownership of religious property is vested in some civil corporation or private person.

As a rule the authors do not oblige religious administrators to follow the prescriptions of canon 534 if the transaction is between units of the same religious institute. In this case they would allow alienations according to the norms of the constitutions.[8] Some, however, hold that the transactions must be between the institute and its subordinate provinces or houses, or between the province and its subordinate houses, otherwise the law of canon 534 obliges.[9] Still others hold that the prescript of canon 534 is of obligation at all times.[10]

2. Under this canon comes all immovable and movable property that is part of the *fixed capital* of the religious moral person. By *fixed capital* is usually understood the property (land or investment) which provides the religious with support and the means of carrying on their work. If this capital is alienated or obligated then the work or the support of the religious is rendered less secure.

By nature food, clothing, farm animals, etc., are consumer goods and not included under the prescripts of alienation. *By destination* money, or even houses and lands may be acquired by the religious to be used as *working capital*, in which case they are not subject to the laws of alienation. In this sense money temporarily on deposit, even though it is bringing in some interest, is not fixed capital. Payments that have been made in kind towards debts owed to the religious do not constitute fixed capital, even though it be a house or a piece of property that has

---

[8] Cf. Larraona, *op. cit.*, XIII (1932), 187, 188; Ferreres, *Las Religiosas*, n. 356.

[9] Cf. Vromant, *op. cit.*, n. 310.

[10] Cf. Bastien, *Directoire canonique*, 1923, n. 514; Ojetti, *Synopsis*, n. 296; Pirhing, lib. III, tit. 13, n. 6.

been given and accepted in payment. Donations, even of immovable property, that are intended to supply daily necessities are not fixed capital.

However, to be considered as fixed capital, subject to the laws regulating alienations, are the following:

a) Money legitimately set aside for the purchase of immovable property or precious movable property. To use this money for any but its intended purpose would be alienation.

b) Money or investments that have been legitimately added to the fixed capital, especially if producing revenue;[11]

c) The increased market-value of investments or of immovable property. (Not to be confused with the interest or dividend.)

d) Money or property received as a pious foundation which has a long-time or perpetual obligation of Masses or other charitable works attached thereto, if the obligations have not yet been fulfilled.

e) Money or property realized from the sale of bonds or debentures on ecclesiastical property in the public market or to private investors.

f) Money or property received under the so-called annuity agreement providing for the payment of an annuity to the donor for life.[12]

g) Money received from the sale of real estate belonging to the fixed capital of the religious moral person.

---

[11] According to Vromant, property becomes *fixed capital* only when made so by an externally manifested act of a competent superior, following, where they exist, the norms of the constitutions. For this reason the fact that the *net yearly surplus* has been fruitfully deposited or reserved for future needs by an econome or by a superior does not necessarily mean that it has been added to the fixed capital, or that it cannot be used or alienated.—*Op. cit.*, n. 280[2]; also Reiffenstuel, lib. III, tit. 13, n. 15.

[12] Letter of the Apostolic Delegate, Wash., D. C., Nov. 13, 1936, nn. I, V; Vromant, *op. cit*, n. 280, 281; Larraona, *op. cit.*, pp. 191-193; Vermeersch-Creusen, *Epitome*, II, n. 861; Schmalzgrueber, lib. III, tit. 13, n. 50.

3. Precious objects are included under the prescripts regulating alienation. A thing is 'precious' if it has a notable value because of the material it contains or because of its artistic or historical worth.[13]

4. Relics and images: Important relics or images of great value, as well as relics and images that are held in great honor by the people in some church, cannot be validly alienated nor can they be permanently transferred to another church without the permission of the Holy See.[14]

B. The Acts Governed by Canon 534

1. The grant or remission of servitudes or easements. A servitude may be defined as a proprietary right vested in a definite person or annexed to the ownership of a definite piece of land, over land or other property belonging to another person, and limiting the enjoyment by that person of his property in a definite manner.[15] A servitude is *active* if it is vested in the religious moral person, allowing the moral person some right over the land of another. It is *passive* if it allows to another some right over the land of the religious moral person. To give up the former or allow the latter is an act regulated by the laws for alienation.

2. Contracts by which the property of the religious moral person is pledged or promised as security for the fulfillment of the contract, thus,

a) Pledge.—When the possession of religious property is handed over to another as security.

b) Mortgage.—When, by a contract, another receives the right to sell or acquire religious property which has been obligated for the acquittal of a debt.[16]

---

[13] Canon 1497 § 2; cf. p. 140 for further explanations.

[14] Canon 1281 § 1; cf. pp. 142-143.

[15] Leage, *Roman Private Law*, p. 177.

[16] By this is meant a special mortgage that arises from a contract between parties; not the general mortgage or lien on property that arises by law

c) Perpetual or Quasi-Perpetual Lease.—By which the use of religious property can not be recovered by the moral person as long as the lessee pays his rent. Another possible danger arising from this contract is that the lessee can sub-let or mortgage the rights acquired by the lease to any one he wishes, unless expressly forbidden by the terms of the lease.[17]

d) The Rental of church property, especially if for more than nine years. This question needs fuller explanation and will be treated later. [18]

e) In General all Acts and Contracts by which ecclesiastical property is exposed to danger or loss, or by which the juridical right of ownership is rendered less secure.[19]

C. The Acts Not Governed by Canon 534

The following acts, even though similar to alienation, are not alienation in the sense of the law.

1. Expenditures made or debts paid with money that does not constitute part of the fixed capital of the moral person.

2. Borrowing or lending money, as long as no contractual obligations burdening the religious property are assumed.[20]

3. Non-acceptance of profit, or of a donation.[21]

---

in regard to the payment of taxes, liability to workmen, etc. Cf. Bastien, *Dir. Can.*, n. 510.

[17] Cf. Leage, *op. cit.*, pp. 188-193. The definitions are adopted from the Roman Law for the reason that the legislator in all probability used this system as a common basis, since it would be impossible to reconcile the variations to be found in the different legal systems in force at present. However, it must be kept in mind that the civil law in each place in regard to contacts and payments that concern ecclesiastical property has the same force as canon law in virtue of canon 1529, and must be observed unless contrary to the divine law or other special prescript of the Code.

[18] Cf. below, pp. 150-151.

[19] Wernz, *Jus Decret.*, III, n. 151; Pejska, *Jus Can. Rel.*, p. 70; Larraona, *op. cit.*, p. 189.

[20] Larraona, *op. cit.*, p. 189; Pejska, *op. cit.*, p. 70.

[21] D'Annibale, *Summula*, III, 80; Vermeersch, *De Religiosis*, I, n. 436.

4. The acquisition of property by 'purchase-money mortgages,' or by mortgages which merely give the holder a claim against the property acquired and not against the one acquiring it.[22]

5. The return of property to the seller if it was purchased with the condition that the seller could buy it back at his option.[23]

6. Custom allows the sale of old church furnishings in order to purchase new furnishings of equal value.[24]

7. The change of investments in stocks, bonds, shares, etc., into other investments equally safe, or the withdrawal of such investments for the purchase of immovable property, is not alienation. Whether the withdrawal of investments for the purpose of putting the money on deposit at interest is alienation or not, is disputed among the authors.[25]

8. The purchase or construction of a dwelling for the religious which it would otherwise be necessary to rent is probably not alienation, even when part of the fixed capital is used for this purpose. The same holds for *necessary* repairs in regard to such buildings. However, this opinion cannot be extended to *im-*

The refusal of a donation made to a moral person is forbidden by canon 1536 paragraph 2. However, the act is not alienation since *acquired* property is not thereby transferred.

[22] Vermeersch, *l.c.*, Leurenius, De Foro Beneficiali, lib. III, q. 151; Vromant, *l.c.;* Bastien, *Dir. Can.*, n. 514. However, this opinion seems to neglect the fact that money paid by the religious moral person on the mortgage, either as interest or part payment of the principal may possibly be lost, if the mortgage has to be foreclosed. Individual cases should be examined cautiously before applying this opinion.

[23] Vermeersch, *l.c.*

[24] Engel, lib. III, tit. 13, n. 5; Reiffenstuel, lib. III, tit. 13, n. 14; Wernz, *Jus Decret.*, III, n. 77; Vermeersch, *l.c.;* D'Annibale, *op. cit.*, n. 77.

[25] Cf. Vermeersch-Creusen, *Epitome,* II, n. 852; Larraona, "Commentarium Codicis," *CpR,* XIII (1932), 192-193.

provements, nor to the extinction of other debts burdening the religious moral person.[26]

N. B.—The above enumeration concerns only alienation. It must not be presumed that permission for investment and expenditures, etc., according to the norms of the Sacred Canons and the constitutions, is unnecessary because not mentioned.

3. GENERAL NORMS FOR ALIENATION AND OBLIGATIONS.

I. *Just Cause*

1. In general, the alienation of church property is not allowed unless there be a just cause requiring it. To be 'just' a cause should be in proportion to the alienation that is to be effected. It need not be a grave cause. The alienation of church property without a just cause will not invalidate the alienation. However, the one doing this is bound to make restitution for any injury resulting to the moral person from his act.[27]

2. Just causes may be classed under the following headings:

a) *Urgent Necessity.*—A necessity is urgent when there is no other way to supply a need except by the alienation of property. If other means are at hand the necessity for alienation is not urgent, and the alienation is not permitted. Instances of urgent need are the necessity to pay debts, to redeem a mortgage, to provide support, to make necessary repairs,[28] provided, in all these cases, there is no other way of accomplishing these things than by alienating church property. The necessity, however,

---

[26] Vromant, *op. cit.*, n. 280; Vermeersch, *De Rel.*, I, n. 439; Pellizarius, *De Monialibus* (Faventiae, 1686), Ch. III, n. 64; S.C.C., 12 July 1919—*AAS*, XI (1919), 418.

[27] Cf. canon 1530 § 1,2°; S.R.R., 9 Aug. 1927—*S.R. Rotae Decisiones*, XIX (1927), dec. XLIV, n. 7; Augustine, *A Commentary*, VI, 595; Larraona, "Commentarium Codicis," *CpR*, XIII (1932), 356.

[28] Cf. above, p. 125, n. 8.

may be either intrinsic or extrinsic in relation to the moral person whose property is to be alienated.[29]

b) *Evident Utility of the Church.*—A just cause for alienation is present if the Church will derive evident utility from the alienation. Circumstances must determine when an alienation of property is useful. Anything that promotes the economic, civil, social, cultural and moral standing of the Church is useful. However, to justify an alienation of property there must be no other available way of accomplishing these ends. Besides this the utility must be evident, leaving no room for doubt. It must be an advantage to the Church, i. e., the Church Universal, the diocese, the parish, religious moral person. An alienation that is profitable to individuals or to some particular activity, is not permitted on the score of usefulness to the Church.[30]

c) *Piety.*—By piety as a just cause for alienation is to be understood all works of religion or of mercy, whether corporal or spiritual. Piety supposes the intention to bring aid in the name of charity or religion to individuals in distress or misfortune or to groups or charitable undertakings in need of aid. The goods of the Church have always been the patrimony of the poor, and the Church has never hesitated to impoverish or even to despoil herself to practice the great precept of charity. When other means are unavailable the alienation of church property has always been permitted in order to succor the needy, to build new churches and schools when necessary, to advance the work of the missions, to purchase burial grounds, etc.[31]

II. *Permission and Consent*

1. No alienation of church property is valid unless the religious administrator has previously obtained the permission of

---

[29] Barbosa, lib. III, c. XXX, n. 12; Reiffenstuel, lib. III, tit. 13, n. 18; Larraona, *l.c.*

[30] C. 1, *De rebus non alien.*, III, 4, *in Clem;* Reiffenstuel, *op. cit.*, nn. 19, 220; Cleary, *Alienation of Church Property*, p. 63.

[31] Cleary, *op. cit.*, p. 64; Vermeersch, *De Religiosis*, II, n. 852.

the legitimate superior. If this permission has been neglected the defect can be rectified only by the Holy See.[82]

2. Only in certain cases does the Code determine this superior:

a) For the alienation of precious objects or of property worth more than six thousand dollars all religious must have the permission of the Holy See. The same is true for contracting debts or obligations of more than six thousand dollars.[83]

b) Sisters of diocesan religious institutes and also nuns must have the permission of their local ordinary, not only for the cases mentioned above, but for other cases involving sums less than six thousand dollars. If the nuns are subject to a regular superior, they must in addition have his permission.

c) Besides the above permissions religious are obliged to obtain the permission of their religious superior. But the Code merely makes mention of this obligation, leaving the determination of the superior in the different cases to the constitutions.[84]

3. It is clear from canon 534 that, in order to alienate property or to contract debts and obligations, the permission of three or four superiors will at times be necessary, and in addition to this the consent of as many or more councils or chapters. Likewise the law requires that the permission be given in writing, and that the consent be manifested by secret vote. As the regulation of alienation is considered of great importance in the Code, it may be asked to what extent these solemnities are required for the validity of the alienation or of the contract?

A. Permission of Superiors.—It is clear from the text of canon 534 that whenever the permission of the Holy See is required the validity of the act depends on obtaining it. Not only this, it must also be obtained prior to the transaction, and the rescript must be properly executed.[85]

---

[82] Canon 1530 § 1,3°; S.C.C., *Albinganen*, 17 May 1919—*AAS*, XI (1919), 386.

[83] This permission should be obtained from the S.C. de Religiosis.

[84] Cf. canon 534 § 1.

[85] Cf. especially canons 39 and 40 regarding the validity of rescripts.

Canonists are unanimous in stating that the permission of the superior, as determined by the constitutions, and likewise the permission of the local ordinary and the regular superior, when this is prescribed by law, are all necessary for the validity of the transaction. Though this is not stated in express terms in canon 534, it is clear from canon 1530 § 1,3°, which all authors apply to religious administrators.

If it be asked whether, in a case where the permission of the Holy See, of the local ordinary, of the regular superior and of the religious superior are required to effect an alienation, it suffices for the validity of the act to have the permission of the highest superior, the answer would seem to be in the negative for the reason that the law does not merely prescribe the permission of the superior, but of the *legitimate* superior. In the case mentioned all four, by prescript either of law or of the constitutions, are legitimately entitled to give the permission, and therefore all four permissions are required for the validity of the act.[86]

B. The Consent of the Council or Chapter.—Canon 534 states that the religious superior who gives permission for alienations or contracts should have the consent of his council or chapter. The particular law of the religious institute will determine whether it is the chapter or the council that is to give the consent in a particular case. In either case, however, a vote should be taken (*per secreta suffragia*), and the will of the council or chapter is determined by the result of the vote.[87] From this it is clear that the superior is not allowed to disregard the vote and merely ask the advice of his chapter or council. The law requires that he have the *consent* of his council or chapter.

---

[86] Cf. Berutti, *Institutiones I.C.*, III, 122. This argument is based on the wording of canon 1530 § 1,3° and refers to careless or culpable neglect in obtaining the required permissions. If the permission were asked directly of the Holy See and reasons stated for omitting other prescripts of the law, the indult, if granted, would of course be valid.

[87] Cf. canon 101.

Without this consent his act is invalid according to the general law stated in canon 105,1°.[38]

C. Written Permission and Secret Vote.—Amongst other formalities canon 534 prescribes that the permission of the superior be obtained in writing and that the consent of the council or chapter be given by secret ballot. A divided opinion exists among the authors as to whether these formalities are prescribed for the validity of the act. Those claiming that they are for validity say it would be arbitrary to separate the "form of the act" from the act itself. Those holding the opposite view maintain that the additional formalities are invoked by the law merely for the sake of supplying proper proof of the transaction and therefore not as a condition for its validity.[39]

Without discussing the merits of these arguments which are rather concerned with the intention of the legislator than with the text of the law itself, it seems that no proof can be deduced from the law itself that these formalities are required for the validity of the act. Lacking this proof the prescript of canon 1680 § 1 is particularly applicable, viz., that "only then should an act be considered null when it lacks essentially constitutive elements, or when solemnities or conditions have been omitted which are prescribed *by the sacred canons under pain of nullity.*" Writing and secrecy are solemnities, but it is not evident that canon 534 prescribes them under pain of nullity, and therefore it would seem that the omission of these solemnities would not nullify the act as far as canon 534 is concerned. However, if the constitutions prescribe them for validity, the constitutions are law in this regard.[40]

---

[38] Cf. Augustine, *A Commentary,* III, 188; Larraona, "Commentarium Codicis," *CpR,* XIV (1933), 179.

[39] *For validity: Larraona,* "Comm. Cod.," *CpR,* XIV (1933), 180; Toso, *Comm. Min.,* lib. II, p. 80; Mayer, *Benediktinisches Ordensrecht,* II, 292.

Not for validity: Blat, *Commentarium,* II, 511; Vromant, *op. cit.,* n. 308[3]. Maroto, *Institutiones,* n. 472; Vermeersch-Creusen, *Epitome,* II, n. 848; a Coronata, *Institutiones,* I, 677; Berutti, *Institutiones,* III, 121.

[40] The Apostolic Delegate in his letter to religious superiors writes: "In

In regard to alienations and contracts it apparently may be considered a practice of the Holy See to insist on the fulfillment of them, even if all the *rigores iuris* have not been observed, provided that the moral person suffers no injury therefrom, and the other party to the contract has been in continuous good faith. This is necessary if the good name of the moral person is to be preserved and the good-will of the laity maintained.[41]

III. *The Petition for Permission*

> § 2. *"In precibus pro obtinendo consensu ad contrahenda debita vel obligationes, exprimi debent alia debita vel obligationes, quibus ipsa persona moralis, religio vel provincia vel domus, ad eum diem gravatur; secus obtenta venia invalida est."*—Canon 534.

Paragraph two of canon 534 may be introduced here to show what is required in the petition for permission to contract debts or obligations. This paragraph requires that in making this petition the petitioner must declare al other debts and obligations with which the moral person he represents is burdened at the time the petition is made. If this is not done the permission if obtained is *invalid.*

1. The source of this prescript makes it clear that all superiors, and not merely the Holy See, when asked to give permission for contracting a debt or obligation, must be informed of the other debts and obligations burdening the moral person at the time the permission is requested.[42] This is also evident from the gen-

regard to other alienations of property which include the incurring of debts or the assuming of obligations for sums smaller than six thousand dollars, the Canon Law provides for certain formalities which should be scrupulously observed."

[41] Cf. S.R.R., 5 July 1927—*S.R. Rotae Decisiones,* XIX (1927), dec. XXXIV, n. 33.

[42] S.C., de Rel., instr. *Inter ea,* 30 July 1909, nn. III, IV—*AAS,* I (1909), 695-699.

eral nature of paragraph two which makes it applicable to all that precedes in paragraph one,[43] and from the letter of the Apostolic Delegate of the United States in his instruction to religious superiors regarding the obligations of canon 534.[44]

2. The information regarding outstanding debts and obligations must be given to the superior granting permission, whenever new debts and obligations are to be contracted. Strictly speaking, this prescript does not require that this information be made available to the superior or to the Holy See when petitioning for permission to alienate property. However, a special law regarding permission to alienate is found in canon 1532 § 4, in virtue of which the petitioner must state in his petition to alienate church property, whether any part or parts of the property to be alienated have already been alienated. Without this statement the permission to alienate, if obtained, is invalid.[45]

3. It is required to inform the superior about other outstanding debts and obligations such as contracts, mortgages, bond issues, debentures etc., but not about rentals, leases, and alienations that have been made, nor about debts or obligations previously contracted but now paid.[46]

The debts and obligations which must be reported are those *actually or contingently* burdening the moral person wishing to

---

[43] Larraona, *op. cit.*, XIV (1933), 252; Blat, *Commentarium,* II, 583; Schoensteiner, *Grundriss des Ordensrechts*, p. 234.

[44] "If the petitioner fails to declare in the petition the debts and obligations which actually encumber the institute, province or religious house for which the indult or permission is sought, canon 534 § 2 of the Code of Canon Law declares the apostolic indult or the *permission of the superior null and void.*"—Cf. Letter, Nov. 13, 1936, n. IV.

[45] Letter of Apostolic Delegate, Nov. 13, 1936, IV, n. 4. Cf. Larraona, *op. cit.*, p. 253.

[46] Current expenses which will certainly be paid at the end of the month or of the year from the regular income are considered as expenses rather than debts. Cf. Vromant, *op. cit.*, n. 309; Creusen, *Het kloosterleven,* n. 130; Larraona, *op. cit.*, p. 253; Berutti, *Institutiones*, III, 121.

contract the new debt. By actual debts and obligations are meant those for which the moral person contracting is directly responsible, even though another in the event of insolvency is responsible as guarantor, bondsman, or co-signor.[47] By contingent obligations are meant those for which the petitioner is not directly responsible, but for which he is responsible as guarantor, surety, trustee, bondsman, co-signor, etc., in the event of the insolvency of another.[48]

4. Besides the above, the following facts, as indicated in the letter of the Apostolic Delegate, must be stated:

> The petition which must be presented to the Holy See, according to the provisions of canon 534, for permission and authorization to incur such obligations, must contain DEFINITE AND CLEAR STATEMENTS OF THE FOLLOWING FACTS:
>
> 1. THE REASON for contracting the debt or assuming the obligation.
>
> 2. The NATURE of the debt or obligation. A mere general statement does not comply with the requirements for an explicit declaration of intention. For example, a mere statement that permission for a loan is required does not satisfy the requirements, if an intention exists to issue bonds or debentures.
>
> 3. The NAME of the person, firm or corporation with whom the debt or obligation is to be contracted.
>
> MOREOVER THE SACRED CONGREGATION REQUIRES THE FOLLOWING ADDITIONAL INFORMATION:
>
> 4. The proposed TERMS of meeting the debt or obligation. This requires a detailed and truthful statement of the arrangements for extinguishing such obligations both as to the interest requirements and the principal debt. This requirement demands a statement of the

[47] It will be opportune in the petition for permission to mention the fact of guarantors or co-signers, so that complete information about the financial condition of the petitioner may be had. Cf. Larraona, *op cit.*, p. 254.

[48] Cf. Letter of the Apostolic Delegate, Nov. 13, 1936, III, n. 4.

time contemplated for complete payment. In this regard, attention is called to canon 536 § 5, which warns superiors not to allow the contracting of debts unless it be certain that the interest on them may be met from CURRENT REVENUE and that WITHIN A REASONABLE TIME THE CAPITAL may be paid off by means of a lawful amortization fund. For example:

a. Loans—the plan of amortization must be presented.

b. Annuities—the amounts, the plan of investing the funds and interest arrangement, and plans for meeting annual payment, etc., must be stated in detail.

5. The ECONOMIC CONDITION of the petitioner, which must be illustrated by the following exhibits:

a. A balance sheet of current assets and liabilities. The value of each asset ought to be stated at the current price, not at the purchase or nominal price; e. g., bonds should be listed at the current quotation on the exchange; real estate should be listed according to the tax assessments, depreciation, income, etc.

b. A statement of receipts and expenditures over a sufficient period of time to give an accurate estimate of normal receipts and expenditures.

c. A separate list of the obligations which do not appear under (a): e. g., obligations as guarantor, surety, trustee, bondsman, etc. This information is required in order to estimate all the certain or contingent obligations of the petitioner, particularly with reference to the rule regarding coalescence.

If the petitioner fails to declare in the petition the debts and obligations which actually encumber the institute, province or religious house for which the indult or permission is sought, CANON 534 § 2 OF THE CODE OF CANON LAW DECLARES THE APOSTOLIC INDULT OR THE PERMISSION OF THE SUPERIOR NULL AND VOID.[49]

---

[49] Letter of the Apostolic Delegate, Nov. 13, 1936, § IV.

IV. *Appraisal of the Object*

1. By affirming in canon 534 the binding force of canon 1531, the legislator prescribes for the act of alienation the necessity of obtaining an appraisal of the value of the object to be alienated. The religious administrator, therefore, is not free to alienate church property at a price determined by himself. In virtue of canon 1530 § 1,1°, the value of the object to be alienated must be determined by experienced men and stated by them in writing.

2. The basis on which the appraisal is to be made is not the absolute value of the object to be alienated but its present market-value. As is clear, this may be either above or below its absolute value.

3. The number of experienced men used in making this appraisal should be at least two. More than two may be used; but one will not suffice.[50] The religious superior who gives consent to the alienation is allowed to designate the experts who are to make the appraisal. He should be convinced of their honesty.[51]

4. The appraisal of the experts must be submitted in writing,[52] and separate appraisals are to be preferred. This and any other precautions deemed necessary may be exacted by the superior. If the appraisal is not satisfactory, the superior may commission other experts to make an appraisal.[53]

5. The object to be alienated must not be sold at a price which is less than the appraisal of the experts, even though the price obtained would still be a just price. If the experts have agreed on a maximum and minimum value for the object to be alienated, the minimum value may be accepted. More than the maxi-

---

[50] Cf. canon 1793 § 3.

[51] Canon 1795 § 1.

[52] S.C. de Prop. Fide, instr. *Ad Patriarch. Armen.*, 30 July 1867, n. 1—*Collectanea*, n. 1310.

[53] Canon 1532 § 2.

mum value may be accepted if no injustice is done thereby.[54] If no buyer can be found at the appraised price of the object to be alienated, the superior may have another appraisal made in order to see if under the circumstances the object may not be sold for less than the former appraised price.

V. *Public Auction*

Paragraph 2 of canon 1531 prescribes that church property should be alienated at a public auction or at least that the fact of alienation should be made known, unless circumstances suggest a different course of action. The object to be alienated should be sold to the one who, all things considered, makes the best offer.

1. The general rule for alienation is that announcement of it should be made in advance, especially to those who might be interested in it, and that the bidding be publicly conducted by an auctioneer.[55] But if a public auction will be in any way disadvantageous to the moral person, it suffices that announcement of the alienation be made to prospective purchasers. In this way the expenses of a public auction are reduced and many of the dangers from trickery, fraud and collusion that accompany public bidding can be avoided.[56] If, however, there is a decided advantage to be gained or a serious disadvantage to be avoided, the religious administrator is allowed to effect the alienation in a strictly private manner by confidential negotiations with one or several indivduals. Such a course may be necessitated by the danger of creating a public scandal, the fear of be-

---

[54] Vermeersch-Creusen, *Epitome*, II, n. 853; Augustine, *A Commentary*, VI, 596; Vromant, *op. cit.*, n. 284 ; De Meester, *Jus Can. Comp.*, III, 1485.

[55] Benedict XIV, motu proprio, *"Essendo,"* 23 Nov. 1742, nn. I, II—*Fontes*, n. 332; S.C. Ep. et Reg., *Aquapenden*, 2 Sept. 1793—*Fontes*, n. 1888; S.C. Ep. et Reg., decr., 18 March 1835—*Fontes*, n. 1905; S.C.C., *Ordinis S. Fran.*, 18 March 1719—*Fontes*, n. 3185.

[56] Larraona, "Commentarium Codicis," *CpR*, XIII (1932), 358.

ing molested by civil authorities, the danger of law suits, taxation, suspicions, calumnies, loss of prestige.[57]

2. The law does not determine who is to decide the manner of alienation that will be best. The superior who has received permission to alienate will in all probability be best acquainted with local conditions and, therefore, there seems to be no reason why the decision should not be left with him. In this however, he should be subject to the superior granting the permission. If an indult to alienate has been received from the Holy See, the one to whom the execution of the rescript has been entrusted should have the right to decide.[58]

3. No matter in what way the alienation is effected, the property should be alienated to the one who, all things being considered, makes the best offer. There is no obligation, therefore, to sell or lease to the highest bidder, unless under the circumstances the highest offer is also the best. The determination of the best offer will depend on the honesty and credit of the bidders; the plan of payment proposed; the time and place of payment; the security of the contract, etc. In a public auction it should be made known that bids will be considered only in the light of these conditions.[59]

VI. *Investment of Proceeds*

> "*Pecunia ex alienatione percepta caute, tuto et utiliter in commodum Ecclesiae collocetur.*"—Canon 1531 § 3.

From this prescript of canon 1531 it is evident that permission to alienate church property does not include *ipso facto* permission to spend or use the money obtained from the alienation.

---

[57] *Ibid.*

[58] Vermeersch-Creusen, *op. cit.*, n. 853; Vromant, *op. cit.*, n. 284; Augustine, *A Commentary,* VI, 596; Larraona, *op. cit.*, p. 358; Cleary, *Alienation of Ch. Prop.*, p. 68.

[59] Larraona, *op. cit.*, p. 359.

There may be cases where alienation takes place without a return of money or property that can be invested. In such cases the prescript does not apply, as is evident. But where money has been realized on an alienation, the superior receiving it has *per se* the obligation to place the money in a safe and profitable investment for the benefit of the moral person whose property has been alienated.[60] It canot be presumed that the cause which justifies alienation, no matter how urgent it may be, justifies the expenditure of the money received.[61] This is allowed only after the legitimate superior has given his consent. In practice, the Sacred Congregation of Religious in granting permission to alienate church property either grants with it permission to spend or use the money realized on the alienation, or reminds the petitioner of the obligation to observe the prescript of canon 1531 § 3.

However, this serves only for indults obtained from the Holy See. What, it may be asked, should be the procedure, if according to the provisions of canon 534 § 1 the permission to alienate has been granted by a superior who is inferior to the Holy See? May that superior also permit the expenditure of the proceeds, or is it necessary for this to obtain the special permission of the Holy See?

Father Larraona is authority for the statement that there is no formula in the Sacred Congregation of Religious for granting permission to spend the proceeds of alienations effected on the authority of religious superiors, for the reason that this permission is never asked for.[62] The only plausible explanation for this is that superiors who give permission to alienate believe that they can also give permission to spend the money realized from the alienation. However, the wonted calm of superiors in this

---

[60] When so prescribed according to the provisions of canon 533, the previous consent of the local ordinary or regular superior must be obtained for this investment.

[61] S.C.C., *Dioecesis N.*, 12 July 1919—*AAS, XI* (1919), 418.

[62] *Op. cit.*, XIII (1932), 360.

matter has been disturbed by the solution of a doubt proposed to the Sacred Congregation of the Council. Explaining the meaning of canon 1531 § 3, it stated in this case that although a Bishop (it could also be a religious superior) can safely give permission to alienate precious objects which do not exceed two hundred dollars (1000 lire) in value without the need of applying to the Holy See, still the solemnities of canons 1530-32 must be observed, and especially canon 1531 § 3; so that to spend or use such money there is *always need of the permission of the Holy See, or of a dispensation from the obligation imposed clearly, explicitly, and without exception by said canon.*[63]

In regard to this explanation of the canon there is the *possibility* that the application was being made merely to the case in question.[64] Since the case concerned the alienation of *votive offerings,* which in no case may be alienated without the permission of the Holy See, there was an obligation to obtain the consent of the Holy See not only to alienate but also to spend the proceeds of the alienation, even though the sum involved was less than two hundred dollars.[65] Added to this possibility is the fact, which cannot be unknown to the Holy See, that the proceeds of numberless alienations for which the permission of the Holy See was not required, have been spent without the permission of the

---

[63] "Quibus positis sequeretur etiam res pretiosas quae mille libellarum valorem non excedunt, alienari ab Ordinariis posse, servatis solemnitatibus praescriptis in can. 1530-1532, ex quibus potissimum atendenda est, ad casum nostrum, clausula can. 1531 § 3; 'Pecunia ex alienatione percepta, *caute, tuto et utiliter in commodum Ecclesiae collectur*'; i. e., pecunia retracta non statim erogari valet in usus etiam pios et necessarios, sed immo conservanda est *ad fructum;* ut ergo erogetur seu consumatur, licet ad amplificandam ecclesiam, ut in casu factum est, necessaria est semper Apostolicae Sedis licentia, seu dispensatione super obligatione hac, quam data lex in laudato canone perspicue et explicite, nullaque concessa exceptione, imponit."—S.C.C., *Dioecesis* N., 12 July 1919—*AAS,* XI (1919), 418.

[64] Cf. the words *"ad casum nostrum," "ut in casu factum est."*

[65] *Op. cit.,* p. 419.

Holy See and the Holy See has given no instructions in the matter. Under the circumstances, then, the solution of Father Larraona is eminently practical, viz., that the superior who permits the alienation of church property may also permit the expenditure of the proceeds provided the cause that justifies the alienation requires this expenditure. When, however, the expenditure is not required, the proceeds must be invested prudently, safely and fruitfully for the benefit of the moral person whose property has been alienated, or for the Church in general.[66]

4. PARTICULAR NORMS FOR ALIENATIONS AND OBLIGATIONS.

I. *Precious Objects*

Canon 534 § 1 prescribes that for the alienation of precious objects the permission of the Holy See is required otherwise the alienation is invalid.

1. Precious objects in the meaning of the Code are those which have a notable value for reasons of art, history or material.[67]

If an object has artistic or historic value, as for example a rare book, wood-carving, painting, etc.,[68] it is considered 'precious,' no matter what the material of which it is made. If it has only a material value, then it is 'precious' only if the material itself is precious, e. g., gold, silver, platinum, precious stones. As is clear, both material and artistic or historic value may be combined in the one object.

The alienation of a precious object, as explained above, is not reserved to the Holy See by canon 534, unless the object also has

---

[66] Larraona, "Commentarium Codicis," *CpR*, XIII (1932), 361.

[67] "Dicuntur . . . pretiosa, quibus notabilis valor sit, artis vel historiae vel materiae causa."—Canon 1497 § 2.

[68] The alienation of relics, *famous* images and paintings, and votive offerings is regulated by special laws. Cf. pp. 142-143.

a *notable* value, for only then is it precious in the meaning of this canon.[69]

2. But what is a *notable* value?

There has been no declaration of the Holy See on this point. When the Sacred Congregation of the Council was asked whether for the alienation of objects that were precious in any sense (*utcumque pretiosarum*) the permission of the Holy See was always necessary or whether an ordinary could permit this within certain limits, the question was referred to the Pontifical Commission for the Interpretation of the Code.[70] However, the Pontifical Commission has not seen fit to give a reply. The reason for this is probably found in the history of the term 'notable value.' Never a subject upon which all were agreed, it was, according to D'Annibale, accepted at about fifty dollars (235 lire) in the 17th century. In the 19th, according to Wernz, it was up to one hundred and fifty dollars (750 lire). In the 20th century many will not admit that an object has notable value till it has reached a value of two hundred dollars.[71] Since it will probably change again, there is reason enough for legislators not making any authentic declaration on this matter.

But notwithstanding the lack of an authentic declaration, it may be considered the *practice* of the Holy See, based on the opinion of authors and on the evident distinction drawn in canon 1532 § 2 between things not exceeding two hundred dollars in value and those exceeding that amount, to consider as of notable value only such precious objects that are in excess of two hundred dollars in value. Thus the permission of the Holy See is required for the alienation of precious objects only when they exceed two hundred dollars in value.[72] For objects of less

---

[69] Cf. S.C.C., *Dioecesis, N.*, 12 July 1919—*AAS*, XI (1919), 417.

[70] S.C.C., 14 Jan. 1922—*AAS*, XIV (1922), 160.

[71] D'Annibale, *Summula*, tom. 3, n. 77, note 6; Wernz, *Jus Decret.*, tom. 3, n. 160, note 140; S.C.C. 12 July 1919—*AAS*, XI (1919), 418.

[72] Cf. S.C.C., 12 July 1919—*AAS*, XI (1919), 418; De Meester, *Juris Can. Comp.*, III, 1487; Cappello, *De Censuris*, n. 406; Cocchi, *Commentarium*, III, 169; Raus, *Institutiones*, n. 237.

value it is required and suffices to have the permission of the legitimate superior according to the norms of the constitutions. These permissions are for the validity of the alienation. The other formalities for alienations in general must also be observed.[73]

II. *The Alienation of Relics and Images*

The law of the Church regarding the alienation of relics and images is stated in canon 1281:

> § 1. *Insignes reliquiae aut imagines pretiosae itemque aliae reliquiae aut imagines quae in aliqua ecclesia magna populi veneratione honorentur, nequeunt valide alienari neque in aliam ecclesiam perpetuo transferri sine Apostolicae Sedis permissu.*

1. IMPORTANT RELICS are relics of the Saints or of the beatified but not relics of those who are merely Venerable or Servants of God. Important relics of the saints or of the beatified are those enumerated in § 2 of canon 1281, viz., the body, the head, the arm, the forearm, the heart, the tongue, the leg,[74] or that part of the body in which the martyr suffered, as long as it is entire and not small.[75]

---

[73] Cf. canon 1530 § 1.1°; Berutti, *Institutiones*, III, 121; above, pp. 126-140.

[74] This must be intact from the knee to the foot. A tibia does not constitute an important relic.—S.R.C., 3 June 1662, ad. 2—*Decreta Authentica*, n. 1234.

[75] It may be noted that important relics, as enumerated above, may not be kept in private dwellings or oratories without the express permission of the local ordinary. Cf. canon 1282 § 1. On the other hand they should not be exposed for public veneration in churches and public oratories unless authenticated by a document of a Cardinal or local ordinary or other ecclesiastical personage having the faculty to do this. Cf. canon 1283 § 1. Relics of the Beatified may be exposed for public veneration only in those churches where the office and Mass of the Beatified may be said, or in

2. Precious Images.—Canon 1280 defines as 'precious' those images which are outstanding because of their antiquity or their artistic value or the veneration which they receive from the people.[76]

3. Highly Venerated Relics and Images.—All relics and images in any church, that are outstanding as objects of the devotion of the faithful even though they are not precious or important in the sense explained above, are subject to the laws regulating their alienation or transfer.[77]

4. This canon extends to all the above mentioned images and relics if they are venerated in a church or a public oratory. Larraona does not think it strictly necessary to apply the prescript of this canon to such relics if venerated in public oratories, on the ground that the canon only mentions churches.[78]

Vromant, on the other hand, would apply it even to semi-public oratories.[79] Canon 1191 § 1 strikes a mean between the two opinions in saying that the same law holds for *public* oratories as for churches.

5. Relics or images, as described above, may not be alienated nor permanently transferred to another church without the permission of the Holy See. *A fortiori* they may not be transferred to private homes or elsewhere. A temporary transfer to another

---

other places with the indult of the Holy See. Cf. canon 1287 § 3. On the feast of the Saint or Beatified the *Credo* is to be recited at Mass if an important relic of the Saint or Beatified is preserved in the church. Cf. Wuest-Mullaney, *Matters Liturgical*, n. 163.

[76] Precious images as described above, if venerated in churches or public oratories are not allowed to be repaired or repainted, even if this be necessary, without the written permission of the local or religious ordinary, who, before granting this permission, is obliged to obtain the opinion of prudent and experienced men. Cf. canon 1280.

[77] According to Vromant (*De Bonis Eccl. Temp.*, n. 295) all relics of our Lord's Passion are to be included under the heading of relics that are highly venerated.

[78] *Op. cit.*, XIII (1932), 353.

[79] *Op. cit.*, n. 295.

church would not be contrary to this canon as long as the return of the relic or image is assured.

III. *The Alienation of Votive Offerings*

For the validity of the alienation of votive offerings the permission of the Holy See is always necessary.

1. Votive offerings are those objects offered by the faithful *ex voto* at the altar or at a shrine or image. The offering is an act of religion, not unlike a sacrifice, for the reason that the donor gives up the ownership of something which he dedicates and consecrates to the service of God or of the saints.[80]

2. The laws affecting votive offerings are:

a) To alienate *any* votive offering the permission of the Holy See must first be obtained.

b) Even if the donor agrees to the future alienation of the votive offering, the permission of the Holy See is necessary to alienate it.

c) All offerings at an altar or an image must be presumed to be votive offerings, unless the contrary intention of the donor is evident.[81]

IV. *Alienating or Obligating Property in Excess of* $6,000

1. In order to alienate property exceeding six thousand dollars in value, or to contract debts or obligations in excess of that amount, the permission of the Holy See is necessary, otherwise the alienation or contract is invalid. It is unimportant whether the property to be alienated or obligated is classified as movable or immovable as long as it is subject to the laws for alienation.[82]

---

[80] S.C.C., *Dioecesis N.*, 12 July 1919—*AAS*, XI (1919), 419. The article should have some intrinsic value. Crutches, braces, cains, etc., that are sometimes left at shrines, are merely indicative of the favors received and can hardly be considered as votive offerings.

[81] S.C.C., 14 Jan. 1922—*AAS*, XIV (1922), 160.

[82] Cf. pp. 120-126.

2. Six thousand dollars represents the appraised value of the object to be alienated, or the actual amount of debt burdening the moral person petitioning for permission to contract a debt or obligation. It should be noted however, that the obligation to obtain the permission of the Holy See exists only when the amount is in excess of six thousand dollars. Instead of $6,000 the Code uses the term 30,000 lire or francs. Authors generally accept these as equivalent sums; and they are so accepted in the letter of the Apostolic Delegate.

> The sum of six thousand dollars should be understood, in connection with the terms of the Code, as the equivalent of thirty thousand lire or francs, and in reference to the value of currency based upon gold in distinction to other currencies, gold coin being the true unit of value. In this connection the value is based upon such stable gold content and rate of exchange.[83]

3. Special faculties, granted to religious superiors to alienate ecclesiastical property with a value in excess of six thousand dollars without permission of the Holy See, are not affected by the prescript of canon 534.[84] Whenever there is urgent necessity or evident advantage, and where delay would be dangerous, Apostolic Delegates have the faculty to permit alienations of ecclesiastical property or of property belonging to pious causes, up to a value of sixty thousand francs for the countries of Europe, and up to one hundred thousand francs ($20,000) outside of Europe.[85]

4. *a*) *In the matter of alienations,* the permission of the Holy See is required in order to alienate at one transaction several articles of ecclesiastical property belonging to the same moral

---

[83] Letter of the Apostolic Delegate, § II, Nov. 13, 1936. Cf. also Cleary, *Alienation of Church Property*, pp. 76-78.

[84] Cf. canon 4.

[85] Cf. *Il Monitore Ecclesiastico*, 1922, p. 200; Bouscaren, *Canon Law Digest*, p. 186.

person when the value of the articles taken together is in excess of six thousand dollars.[86]

b) *In the matter of debts and obligations*:

An apostolic indult is required not only in the event of a single transaction exceeding the sum of $6,000, but an apostolic indult is necessary in every case where a coalescence of the debts or obligations of every kind and nature exceeds the said sum of six thousand dollars. For example:

1. If after having contracted a loan of four thousand dollars, an occasion arises for borrowing a further sum of more than two thousand dollars before payment of the first has been made by the religious—since the total of the financial obligations will exceed six thousand dollars after the second borrowing, it is necessary to have the permission of the Holy See before incurring the second loan. This permission is required whether the proposed increase in indebtedness is by contract, mortgage, bond or debenture issue, or any other form which will bring the actual or contingent obligations to a total sum of more than six thousand dollars.

2. When the total present indebtedness is over six thousand dollars,, an apostolic indult is required for any contract, debt or other obligation, even if such new indebtedness is incurred for the purpose of complete or partial payment of the pre-existing debts or obligations.[87]

5. The permission of the Holy See must be obtained prior to the alienation or contract. Religious should send their petition to the Sacred Congregation for Religious. *However, it must not be thought that by giving permission to alienate or to con-*

---

[86] Comm. Pont., 20 July 1929, V—*AAS*, XXI (1929), 574.

[87] Letter of the Apostolic Delegate, § III, Nov. 18, 1936. It should be noted that the obligations stated above are much stricter than those ordinarily stated by canonists. Cf. Goyeneche, "Consultationes," *CpR*, III (1924), 395; Creusen, *Het Kloosterleven*, n. 130.

tract debts the Holy See accepts responsibility for the transaction. The *Beneplacitum Apostolicum* is the mere removal of a canonical hindrance allowing the religious themselves to proceed with the transaction. It does not create an obligation on their part to do so, but merely removes any obstacles which the law may have interposed.[88] To avoid any mistaken notions in regard to this, the Holy See has since 1932 discontinued issuing rescripts, and instead grants the permission in the form of a letter. This letter expressly excludes any economic, moral, or civil obligations on the part of the Sacred Congregation of Religious or of the Holy See.[89]

6. Besides the above rules, the general norms for alienations and contracts, where applicable, must be observed.[90] Special attention should be paid to the statement of other outstanding debts and obligations which must accompany the petition.[91]

V. *Bonds and Annuities*

Under this heading will be treated certain regulations which have been made known to religious superiors of the United States by the Apostolic Delegate in a letter of November 13, 1936. The letter is used almost verbatim.

Two methods sometimes used by religious moral persons for obtaining money are:

1. The issuance of bonds or debentures upon ecclesiastical property, and the sale of such bonds or debentures in the public market or to private investors.

2. The solicitation or acceptance of funds under the so-called annuity agreement by which the recipient of the funds promises or contracts to pay to the donor a life-time annuity.

---

[88] S.C. de Rel., *Dioecesis seu Ordinis N.*, 18 Aug. 1914—*AAS*, VII (1915), 110.

[89] Larraona, "Commentarium Codicis," *CpR*, XIV (1933), 29, 44.

[90] Cf. above, pp. 126-140.

[91] Cf. above, pp. 131-134.

Both of these systems of obtaining money fall within the provisions of canon 534. For under both systems the moral religious person, who issues the bonds or debentures or accepts the funds under an annuity agreement, undertakes economic obligations which must be met at a certain time.

Any religious institute, province or house wishing to issue bonds or debentures or to accept annuities involving a sum exceeding six thousand dollars must obtain the previous permission of the Holy See; otherwise the transaction is both unlawful and invalid.

The apostolic indult is required not only in the event of a single transaction exceeding the sum of six thousand dollars, but also in every case where a coalescence of the sums or obligations resulting from two or more transactions of the same or different kind exceeds the said sum of six thousand dollars. Thus:

1. If a religious moral person undertakes several issues of bonds or debentures, each issue not exceeding the sum of six thousand dollars, but the total of all the issues being in excess of six thousand dollars, then an apostolic indult must be obtained.

2. If a religious moral person under annuity agreements has received from the same or different persons money or property to the value of six thousand dollars, then no further money or property may be accepted under this system without an apostolic indult.

3. If funds already accepted by transactions under either or both of the systems mentioned above total six thousand dollars, no further transactions may be carried on under either system until an apostolic indult has been obtained.

4. If the sum involved in any transaction in either or both of the systems mentioned above, when added to other outstanding debts and obligations, results in a total in excess of six thousand dollars, an apostolic indult is needed to make the transaction.

Regarding the information which must appear in the petition to the Holy See, see pages 131-136.

In particular, however, with regard to annuity funds, it should be noted that "in order to avoid the serious inconveniences and evils when religious institutes imprudently contract obligations under annuity agreements and later are not in a position to satisfy the annuity requirements, it is strictly and formally forbidden to use all or any part of the capital annuity fund which should remain intact as long as the annuitant is living."[92]

VI. *Alienations and Obligations not in Excess of* $6,000

For the alienation of property having a value not in excess of six thousand dollars, or for contracting debts or obligations not beyond that amount, it is required and suffices to have the written permission of the superior according to the norms of the constitutions, and with the consent of the council or chapter manifested by secret votes. Nuns or sisters of diocesan right must also have the written consent of the local ordinary and of the regular superior, if the monastery of nuns is subject to him.

The above prescripts apply to all alienations, debts, and obligations, even those in excess of six thousand dollars. However, for sums in excess of that amount other prescripts of law must also be observed.[93] For sums not in excess of six thousand dollars the fulfillment of the above prescripts is required and suf-

---

[92] Letter of the Apostolic Delegate, § V, Nov. 13, 1936.

NOTE.—This regulation has, undoubtedly, been called forth because of the unsafe and imprudent methods of financing adopted by some who have issued annuity bonds. For these it is necessary. Others, however, who have followed a safe system of financing and have a sufficient reserve fund securely invested, will find it somewhat of a hardship, since it obliges them not only to preserve intact the whole annuity capital, but even to add to it, in order to meet the interest payments on the annuity bonds. Perhaps the Holy See would grant a dispensation from this regulation if a safe plan of administration and investment were submitted to It.

[93] Cf. above, pp. 144-147.

fices. Since it has already been stated that the permission of the Holy See is required for the alienation of precious objects of notable value ($200),[94] it follows that the fulfillment of the prescripts mentioned here is required and suffices when the value is not notable.

As already stated, the consent of the legitimate superior is required for the validity of the act.[95] The questions concerning the written consent of a higher superior, the consent of the council or chapter, given by a secret ballot, and whether or not these things affect the validity or the licitness of the act, have all been discussed under the general norms.[96]

VII. *Renting and Leasing*

RENTING.—Renting is a bilateral contract by which the use of property is permitted to another for a determined period in consideration of a determined price.[97] The special rules for the renting of ecclesiastical property, which must also be observed by religious are as follows:

1. The prescripts of canon 1531 § 2 must be observed, i. e., the property should be rented at a public auction, or at least public notice should be given that the property is for rent, unless circumstances suggest otherwise. The property should be rented to the one who. all things being considered, makes the best offer.[98]

2. Besides the above, the contract of renting should contain the following conditions: (*a*) The boundaries of the property should be exactly designated; (*b*) Cultivation of the land should be in such a manner as not to render it sterile or useless for further cultivation; (*c*) The rental should be paid at the speci-

---

[94] Cf. above, pp. 140-142.

[95] Cf. above, pp. 128-129.

[96] Cf. above, pp. 126-131.

[97] Pirhing, lib. III, tit. 17 n. 1; Vromant, *op. cit.*, n. 335.

[98] Cf. above, pp. 136-137.

fied times and in the way specified; (*d*) Guarantees should be given for the fulfillment of the above conditions.[99]

3. To rent for a period longer than nine years property that will bring in a yearly rental in excess of six thousand dollars, the permission of the Holy See is necessary for the validity of the act.[100]

4. To rent property for periods not in excess of nine years, even if the rental is in excess of six thousand dollars; or to rent property for periods in excess of nine years, provided the rental is not in excess of six thousand dollars, the permission of the legitimate superior according to the norms prescribed by particular law must be obtained.[101]

LEASES.—The difference between renting and leasing is that either movable or immovable property can be rented, but only immovable property can be leased. By renting the tenant only acquires a right to use the property; by leasing the useful ownership of the property is acquired by the lessee so that only the radical ownership remains to the lessor. Moreover the lease runs for a much longer time and does not necessarily expire with the death of the lessee.[102]

Leasing as contemplated by the Code is not usual in the United States. However, any renting for a period longer than nine years is for practical purposes a lease. As far as religious are concerned the laws governing renting and leasing are the same.[103] However, if the act called "redemption of the canon"

[99] Canon 1541 § 1.

[100] Canon 1541 § 2,1°. The return or the rental from the property, not the value of the property itself, determines the necessity of the permission. The rental is considered on a yearly basis; though in some cases, e. g., where certain crops can be gathered only every other year, a bi-yearly basis is allowd. Cf. Vermeersch-Creusen, *Epitome*, II, n. 862. Eichmann, "Ueber den Begriff 'Mietwert [valor locationis]' in C.I.C."—*Theologie und Glaube*, XXIV (1932), 588-592.

[101] Vromant, *op. cit.*, n. 340; Berutti, *Institutiones*, III, 120 note. 1.

[102] Vromant, *op. cit.*, n. 341; Cleary, *Alienation of Ch. Prop.* p. 96.

[103] Cf. Vromant, *op. cit.*, n. 342.

takes place, i. e., if instead of a yearly sum or rental (the canon), the lessor accepts a lump sum, the act is equivalent to an alienation and the prescripts of canon 534 are all applicable.[104] The sum accepted as redemption of the canon must be at least the equivalent of the rental that would have been received.[105]

5. PENALTIES.

1. The omission of anything essential to the act, or of formalities or solemnities which are prescribed for the validity of alienations or for contracting debts or obligations, results in the absolute invalidity of the act.[106] This invalidity cannot be sanated by any but the Holy See. Neither can a convalidation of invalid acts result from performing a new act with retroactive effect. The sanation must be asked of the Holy See. Superiors of a lower order than the Holy See cannot remedy invalid acts resulting from the omission of those things prescribed by common law for validity. Thus, if the permission of the provincial superior is required, only the Holy See, and not the provincial himself, can remedy an act performed without this permission.[107]

2. If an alienation or a contract has been entered into without the observance of the solemnities required by law, the moral person injured thereby has the right, through its legitimate representatives (can. 1649), to enter a personal action, or suit (*actio personalis*) against the guilty party or his heirs for the recovery of the damages. If the alienation, debt, or obligation is invalid, a real action or property suit (*actio realis*) for the recovery of the property may be filed by the alienator, his successor, superior, or any member of the injured moral person,

---

[104] *Ibid.*

[105] Canon 1542 § 1.

[106] Cf. canons 11; 534 § 1; 1530 § 1,3°; 1680 § 1.

[107] Cf. S.C.C., *Albinganem.*, 17 May 1919—*AAS*, XI (1919), 385, 386; cf. above, p. 128.

against anyone possessing the property as a result of the invalid act.[108]

3. Religious, including superiors (even ordinaries) and officials, who presume to alienate or to consent to the alienation of church property contrary to the prescriptions of canon 534 § 1 are liable to the following penalties:[109]

A. Penalties that are incurred *ipso facto* (*latae sententiae*).

If a precious object of notable value ($200), or other property having a value in excess of six thousand dollars is alienated without the consent of the Holy See, the delinquent, who knowingly neglected to obtain the permission of the Holy See and also those who, knowing of this neglect, were in any way guilty of the alienation, either by handing over or receiving the property or by giving consent to the alienation, incur *ipso facto* an excommunication reserved to no one.[110]

B. Penalties that are to be inflicted (*ferendae sententiae*).[111]

1. If the sum involved is not in excess of two hundred dollars, the legitimate superior should inflict suitable penalties.[112]

---

[108] The purchaser may in turn bring action against the one who sold the property. Cf. canons 1534, 536 § 4; 1622.

[109] Provided their consent was efficacious in producing the effect, and they themselves gravely culpable. Cf. Vromant, *op. cit.*, n. 303; Cipollini, *De Censuris*, n. 86; canons 2202 § 2; 2218 § 2; 2347.

[110] Canon 2347,3°. Since the excommunication is reserved to no one, those who have incurred it, as soon as they are penitent and rightly disposed, can be absolved by any priest legitimately approved for confessions. Any ignorance, either of the law or of the penalty which is not an affected ignorance, excuses from the penalty; so also, any fear, duress, influence or circumstance—slight though it be—that lessens the imputability. Cf. canon 2229; Cappello, *De Censuris*, n. 415.

[111] It is allowed to the superior to temper the severity *of ferendae sententiae* penalties, or to inflict in their stead some penal remedy or penance, if there are circumstances which notably lessen the delinquent's imputability. Cf. canon 2223 § 3,3°; Vromant, *op. cit.*, n. 304.

[112] Cf. canon 2223 § 3,3°.

2. If the sum involved is more than two hundred but less than six thousand dollars, a religious superior or econome if delinquent must be deprived of office and of the right to hold office and subjected to other suitable punishments by the competent superior.[113]

The following excerpt from the Letter of the Apostolic Delegate to religious superiors should clear up any doubts about the applicability of the above mentioned penalties to those who contract debts or obligations contrary to the prescriptions of canon 534:

> Finally, I am instructed to advise all religious that the Sacred Congregation, whenever the case requires it and according to the circumstances of each case, will impose upon the transgressors of the above requirements of the Canon Law the sanctions of canon 2347 and other severe penalties according to their discretion, not excluding the penalty of privation of office.[114]

---

[113] Punishments that suppose jurisdiction in the external forum such as suspension and excommunication, can only be inflicted by local or religious ordinaries, i. e., the major superiors of exempt clerical institutes. Religious superiors who are not ordinaries can only punish by deprivation of office, or by retreats, fasts, etc. Cf. D'Annibale, *Summula,* I, n. 324; Bastien, *Dir. Can.,* n. 388; Vromant, *op. cit.,* n. 304.

[114] Letter § V.

CHAPTER V

THE ACCOUNT OF ADMINISTRATION

1. GENERAL NOTIONS.

Since the ownership of church property is vested in ecclesiastical moral persons incapable of acting for themselves, it is necessary that the administration of this property be confided to physical persons known as administrators, superiors, officials. But as the duty of an administrator is to keep an account of his acts and render it to the one whose business is being conducted,[1] it has been a general law in the Catholic Church that all administrators of church property must render an account of their administration, either directly or indirectly, to the Holy See, under whose authority all church property is held.[2] The operation of this law is seen especially in religious institutes wherein by law, each unit must have its econome for the administration of temporalities.[3] The econome must give an account of his administration to his local superior; the local superior to the provincial superior; the provincial to the general superior; and in the quinquennial report the general superior renders an account of the whole institute directly to the Holy See, if the institute is of pontifical right.[4] If the institute is of diocesan right, each house must render an account to the local ordinary of the place where the house is located. In addition to this accounting to the proper superiors of the institute, religious are sometimes obliged by law to give an account to a superior external to their institute, usually the local ordinary, or a regular superior in the case

[1] D. (27, 3) 3.

[2] Canon 1499 § 2.

[3] Canon 516 § 2, cf. p. 90.

[4] Cf. canon 510.

of female religious. In regard to the local ordinary this account is required either because the religious themselves are subject to the local ordinary, e. g., all diocesan religious, or because the property which the religious administer is under the jurisdiction of the local ordinary, since within his territory the local ordinary has the right of supervision over all ecclesiastical property which has not been withdrawn from his jurisdiction.[5]

The way in which the local ordinary may exercise his jurisdiction is determined by law. Over religious of diocesan right he has plenary jurisdiction;[6] over religious of pontifical right he has no jurisdiction in economic matters, except as expressed in canons 533-535;[7] over exempt religious, only that jurisdiction which the law gives him expressly.[8]

As to the nature of the account to be given to the local ordinary general ideas already have been given[9] It was stated that a mere financial statement is not sufficient for an accounting. In the fulfillment of his office the local ordinary is entitled to examine not only the books in which the accounts are kept but also all documents and papers such as contracts, receipts of payments, bank accounts, etc., that will help in clarifying and certifying the truth of the entries in the account books. These books should contain no padding or "doctoring." Each entry should be a true and exact statement of the transaction that has taken place. As to the number of books and the method of keeping them, the religious should conform to the diocesan regulations at least in regard to the books which the local ordinary may examine.[10]

---

[5] Canon 1519 § 1; cf. canon 535.

[6] Cf. Leo XIII, const. *"Conditae a Christo,"* 8 Dec. 1900, Part I, n. X—*Fontes,* n. 644; canon 535 § 3,1°.

[7] Canon 618 § 2,1°.

[8] Canon 615.

[9] Cf. above, pp. 87-88.

[10] Cf. S.C.C., *Ariminen.,* 27 Jan. 1748—*Fontes,* n. 3600; Pallottini, *Collectio,* XV, "redditio rationum," n. 57; S.R.R., 20 Feb. 1913—*S.R. Rotae Decisiones,* V (1913), dec. XV, nn. 5, 9.

The local ordinary may examine the account books as often as the law or the constitutions of the various institutes allow, and regardless of whether the religious themselves or seculars are the administrators.[11] The examination may be made personally or by delegate; but in neither case may a fee be charged for the work which this entails. The account books need not be examined at the religious house. For this purpose the local ordinary may require that they be sent to his residence. However, a minor official cannot be required to produce these books for examination by the bishop, if the superior of the house has not been advised. When the administrator has satisfied the obligations of law or of the constitutions in regard to the account to be rendered to the local ordinary, he should not be again required to make this accounting till the appointed time arrives, unless an error or omission is evident. Neglect on the part of the bishop to demand this account never creates a right to exemption therefrom. In fact the present law places on the religious the obligation to give the account unasked.[12]

2. PARTICULAR NORMS.

I. *Account by Nuns*

§ 1. "*In quolibet monialium monasterio etiam exempto:*

1°. *Administrationis ratio, gratis exigenda, reddatur semel in anno, aut etiam saepius si id in constitutionibus praescribatur, ab Antistita Ordinario loci, itemque*

---

[11] Cf. below, pp. 158, 161, 164.

[12] Cf. canon 535 § 1,2°; Gregory XV, const. "*Inscrutabili,*" 5 Feb. 1622. n. 5—*Fontes,* n. 199; S.C. Ep. et Reg., *Spalaten.,* 9 March 1593—*Fontes,* n. 1478; *Camerinen.,* 9 Dec. 1740, n. 3—*Fontes,* n. 1858; S.C.C., *Neapolitana,* 11 March 1673, n. 1—*Fontes,* n. 2830; *Hieracen.,* 26 Jan. 1692, n. 2—*Fontes,* n. 2925; *Ariminen.,* 2 and 16 Dec. 1747, 27 Jan. 1748, nn. 8, 9—*Fontes,* nn. 3598, 3600; *Conversana,* 13 March, 24 April, 8 May, 1751, n. 23—*Fontes,* n. 3613; Pallottini, *Collectio,* XV, "redditio rationum," nn. 57, 58, 63.

Superiori regulari, si monasterium sit eidem subiectum."—Canon 535.

1. This prescript concerns only nuns, i. e., female religious whose vows are actually solemn or at least solemn *ex instituto,* even though actually simple in virtue of a prescript of the Holy See.[13] It does not matter whether they are exempt or not, nor whether they are subject or not to a regular superior.[14]

2. An account of the entire financial administration of the monastery is required. If the bishop sends out blank forms to be filled in, his regulations in this regard must be complied with; otherwise the method of rendering this account is left to the constitutions or the judgment of the superioress. If forms are not sent out by the local ordinary, the questions to be answered by pontifical institutes in the quinquennial report to the Holy See will undoubtedly be found helpful in making the report to the local ordinary.[15] The account, as a rule, is drawn up by the econome but must be signed by the superioress and her consultors and presented by the superioress to the local ordinary or his delegate.

3. This account must be rendered to the local ordinary at least once a year. If he does not demand it, it must be sent to him for the Code speaks of the obligation of the superioress to render this account and not merely of the right of the ordinary to demand it. If the constitutions of the religious institute oblige the superioress to render this account at more frequent intervals, she must follow the constitutions.

4. If the monastery is subject to a regular superior, the regular superior has the same right to receive an account of the ad-

---

[13] Canon 488, 7°, cf. p. 96.

[14] An interesting account of the status of "nuns" in the United States is contained in Augustine, *A Commentary,* III (ed. 1929), 472-476.

[15] For the English version of these questions cf. *AAS,* XV (1923), 462-464.

ministration as the local ordinary.[16] If the constitutions prescribe two accounts yearly for the local ordinary, this prescription does not extend to the regular superior unless he has been expressly included in it. Nor would such a prescription extend to the right of the local ordinary if made in regard to the regular superior.[17] When the nuns are subject to a regular superior, the local ordinary must advise the regular superior of his intention to examine the accounts and give him an opportunity to be present. If he neglects to be there, the ordinary may proceed alone.[18]

> § 1. "*In quolibet monialium monasterio etiam exempto*:
>
> 2°. *Si ratio administrationis Ordinario non probetur, ipse potest opportuna remedia adhibere, etiam removendo, si res postulet, oeconomam aliosque administratores; quod si monasterium sit Superiori regulari subiectum, eum Ordinarius, uti prospiciat, moneat; quod si ille neglexerit, ipse per se consulat.*"—Can. 535.

Since the right to demand the rendering of accounts of the administration granted by the law to certain superiors external to the religious institutes is for the purpose of safeguarding the property of the Church, it is evident that the right should extend not only to the receiving of accounts and examining them, but also to providing remedies and corrections whenever these are necessary. This is especially true in regard to nuns, who, because of the law of the cloister, are generally unable to support themselves, and for whom, therefore, the loss of what they have acquired by donations, dowries, etc., for their support would lead to grave consequences. Formerly, when lay administrators

---

[16] Commis. Pont., 24 Nov. 1920—*AAS*, XII (1920), 575.

[17] Larraona, "Commentarium Codicis," *CpR.*, XIV (1933), 346.

[18] S.C. Ep. et Reg., *Camerinen.*, 9 Dec. 1840—*Fontes*, n. 1858; S.C.C., *Hieracen.*, 26 Jan. 1692—*Fontes*, n 2925; *Ariminen.*, 27 Jan. 1748—*Fontes*, n. 3600.

were sometimes appointed to administer the property of the monastery, this was more necessary than at present, and a rigorous law in this regard was enacted by Pope Gregory XV, in his constitution "*Inscrutabili.*"[19] However, the Code continues in substance the law of Pope Gregory, and embodies it in the prescript quoted above.

The reasons why a local ordinary may disapprove of the accounts that have been submitted to him for examination may be manifold. Thus, the remedy he applies need not always be a penalty. Since his responsibility is to safeguard the property of the monastery, he is at liberty to provide remedies no matter what the cause that makes them necessary. The remedies may amount merely to suggestions or precepts regarding the mode of administration for the future; but if necessary, the local ordinary may also decree that the econome or other administrators be removed. In applying remedies, if the monastery is directly subject to the local ordinary, he himself may give the necessary orders. If, however, it is subject to a regular superior, the ordinary should first tell the regular superior to provide a remedy. If the latter refuses or neglects to do so, the ordinary himself is at liberty to act. It would seem from this that the judgment about the suitableness of the remedy is left to the bishop, and if he orders the removal of the administrator, the regular superior must obey. Recourse, to be sure, is allowed to the Holy See. But until the Holy See decides, the orders of the Bishop must be followed. The fact that the local ordinary has ordered the removal of an administrator, does not give him the right to choose a successor to that administrator. The norms of the constitutions must be followed in regard to this. However, for obvious reasons the bishop would be allowed to state certain qualifications that the successor must have. The regular superior need not wait for the orders of the local ordinary, but

[19] 5 Feb. 1622—*Fontes*, n. 199.

can on his own initiative provide remedies, even to the extent of removing the administrator.[19*]

II. *Accounts of the Dowries*

> § 2. *"In aliis mulierum religionibus, ratio administrationis bonorum quae dotes constituunt. Ordinario loci reddatur occasione visitationis et etiam saepius, si Ordinarius id necessarium duxerit."*—Canon 535.

It has already been stated that in all monasteries of nuns the dowry is necessary by precept of law, but that in other institutes of simple vows the constitutions alone determine the necessity of the dowry.[20] In the account that is demanded of nuns, an account of the dowry is included. Hence nuns must give an account of the administration of the dowry to the local ordinary at least once a year. In all other religious institutes of women in which the constitutions require that postulants bring a dowry, an account of the administration of the fund which constitutes the dowry of the religious must be rendered to the local ordinary at least at the time of his visitation,[21] or even oftener if the local ordinary judge it to be necessary.

This account when submitted, will, of course, furnish the ordinary the needed opportunity to inquire into the mode of investment of the dowry and the means employed to safeguard the capital. The requirements of the Code in this regard have already been treated, and need not be considered here.[22]

The superioress obliged to give this account to the local ordinary is the provincial or general superioress, since the Code prescribes that the administration of the dowry be conducted at the habitual residence of the general or provincial superioress.[23]

[19*] Larraona, *op. cit.*, p. 348.

[20] Canon 547. Cf. pp. 97-102.

[21] Every five years. Cf. canon 512 § 2,3°.

[22] Cf. above, pp. 97-102.

[23] Canon 550 § 1.

The reason for this prescript is evidently to place the responsibility for the administration of the dowries on the superioresses mentioned, and therefore it seems improbable that the Code sanctions the administration of the dowries by the local superioress at the general's or provincial's place of residence.

The rendering of this account would be facilitated if the administration of the dowry was conducted separately from that of other provincial property. This procedure is apparently indicated as necessary for pious foundations and legacies with obligations of masses or charitable works, and would seem to have its advantages if followed in regard to dowries, especially in pontifical institutes that are not obliged to give an account of all financial matters at the time of visitation.[24]

III. *Accounts by Diocesan Houses*

> § 3. *"Loci Ordinario ius insuper esto cognoscendi:*
> 1°. *De rationibus oeconomicis domus religiosae iuris dioecesani."*—Canon 535.

This prescript refers only to religious of diocesan right, i. e., to those religious institutes which owe their existence to the sole authority of a local ordinary and have not yet obtained approbation or a decree of praise from the Holy See.[25] However, it refers to *all* such institutes of men or women religious alike, even if they have established houses in several dioceses. The local ordinary of each diocese has the right to know about the financial condition of all the houses within his territory.

The norm set down here is not exactly the right of visitation. Visitation (*jus visitandi*) is not excluded by this prescript. But the prescript has reference only to financial matters and is a right which the local ordinary may exercise as often as he deems it necessary. For this end he may examine account

[24] Cf. S.C. de Rel., instr. March 25, 1922, n. 58—*AAS,* XV (1923), 463.
[25] Canon 488,3°.

books and ask to see all documents that will give him information on this subject.

The question arises: Does this right of the local ordinary extend merely to the individual houses of the diocesan institute, or also to the institute itself or provinces thereof, if there be any?

Many authors hold that it extends to the whole institute.[26] It has been objected to this view that the text of the Code speaks of houses, not of provinces or institutes, and that analogical and historical reasons, together with the continuous traditions of the law, favor a restricted interpretation applicable only to houses.[27]

Whatever be the value of these latter reasons, there may be offered in opposition to them:

1. The *logical* reason, that the right stated in this prescript is a consequence of the authority of the local ordinary over diocesan houses. But since the ordinary has as much authority over the institute confined to his territory as he has over the house, his right cannot be limited to the house alone. If the institute is spread into several dioceses the bishops may find it convenient or necessary to delegate one of their number to act for the rest in specified matters. But the necessity of doing this can hardly be considered as establishing a right on the part of the diocesan institute to be free from all supervision in those matters which go beyond the limits of individual houses.

2. The *practical* reason, that diocesan congregations, more than pontifical congregations, need the supervision of an external authority. Yet by restricting this prescript to houses alone, the more important part of the government of diocesan institutes is deprived of this aid.

---

[26] Cf. Chelodi, *Ius de Personis*, p. 436; Schaefer, *De Religiosis*, p. 345; Vermeersch-Creusen, *Epitome*, I, n. 610; Wernz-Vidal, *Jus Canonicum*, III, 184.

[27] Larraona, *op. cit.*, pp. 416-418.

IV. *Accounts of Foundations and Legacies*

§ 3. "*De administratione fundorum legatorumque de quibus in can.* 533 § 1, *nn.* 3, 4."—Canon 535.

The administration of foundations and legacies has been sufficiently treated in the commentary of canon 533. Here it need only be added that the local ordinary in the exercise of his right to keep informed of the administration of this kind of property may examine the account of it as often as he deems it necessary.[28]

[28] Cf. above, p. 112; Leo XIII, "*Conditae a Christo,*" 8 Dec. 1900, § II, n. IX—*Fontes,* n. 644.

CHAPTER VI

RESPONSIBILITY FOR DEBTS AND OBLIGATIONS

Canon 536

1. RESPONSIBILITY OF RELIGIOUS MORAL PERSONS.

The special object of canon 536 is to establish the responsibility for debts and obligations contracted by religious and by religious moral persons. It should be noted that the former law according to which the monastery and not the regular was responsible in civil cases for all debts, even those contracted without permission, has been profoundly modified by the Code.[1]

> § 1. *"Si persona moralis (sive religio, sive provincia, sive domus) debita et obligationes contraxerit etiam cum Superiorum licentia, ipsa tenetur de eisdem respondere."*—Canon 536.

1. This prescript extends to all debts and obligations which have been contracted in the name of a religious moral person by those who legitimately represent it. The Code by way of example mentions the institute ,province and house; but the prescript applies equally to other religious moral persons whether collegiate or non-collegiate (canon 99) that have been legitimately erected (can. 100 § 1), provided that particular law has not prohibited nor restricted the moral person's capacity to contract debts and obligations.[2] If a debt or obligation has been contracted with due authorization by the superior of a house which according to the constitutions lacks capacity to acquire or

[1] Larraona, "Commentarium Codicis," *CpR,* XIV (1933), 420.

[2] Cf. canon 531

possess property, then the superior must be considered as the agent of the next higher moral person having this capacity.[3] If the whole order is incapable of owning property, then it is to be understood that each moral person administers the property in its possession in the name of the Holy See and also accepts the responsibility.[4]

2. A religious cannot be said to be the legitimate representative of a moral person unless:

a) He is a superior or an official designated by the constitutions, or a rightful delegate of either of them, and acts within the limits of his office;[5]

b) Nothing essential to the act or expressly prescribed for its validity has been omitted.[6]

3. Even though a higher superior, not a member of the community or moral person contracting the debt or obligation, has given his permission for the transaction, the responsibility for the transaction remains with the moral person contracting. This is true even though the permission was necessary for the validity of the act. As already stated, this permission is a mere removal of a canonical hindrance and is not a permission to contract in the name of the superior or the moral person he represents, but only a permission to contract in the name of the petitioner.[7]

4. This prescript is intended to fix both canonical and civil responsibility. It may happen however, that a transaction is canonically invalid and civilly valid. The civil validity of itself does not obligate the moral person. If compelled to assume the

---

[3] Schaefer, *De Religiosis*, p. 345; Pruemmer, *Manuale J.C.*, q. 197.

[4] Oesterle, *Praelectiones J.C.*, p. 280-281; Larraona, *op. cit.*, p. 421.

[5] Canon 532 § 2.

[6] Canon 1680 § 1. An invalid act is no act; therefore the moral person cannot be held responsible. Cf. S.C.C., *Albinganen.*, 17 May 1919—*AAS*, XI (1919), 383.

[7] Cf. S.C. de Rel., *Dioecesis seu Ordinis N.*, 18 Aug. 1914—*AAS*, VII (1915), 110. Cf. above, p. 146.

responsibility, the moral person has the right to an action for damages against the one causing them.[8]

5. The important consequence that flows from this law is that even in centralized religious institutes, where all are subject to the general superior, and where houses have a subordinate position in relation to the province, and provinces in relation to the institute, one moral person cannot be held responsible for the debts or obligations of another. Thus, where each has separate capacity, the province cannot be held responsible for the debts of the house, nor the house for those of the province. This is the conclusion to be drawn from the common law of the Church, which in this matter emphasizes the juridical and economic independence of the moral persons. Constitutions, however, are not to be considered as contrary to this prescript of the Code if they allow the provincial superior to obligate the goods of a house in transacting affairs of the province. Such an arrangement does not make the house responsible for all contracts made in the name of the province, but only to the extent that the provincial superior has explicitly and expressly exercised the power granted him by the constitutions.[9] Similarly the province is not responsible for the debts of the house except to the extent that provincial superiors have guaranteed or otherwise accepted responsibility for them. But again be it noted that no responsibility is accepted by the mere grant of permission, no matter how necessary the permission is for the validity of the transaction.

6. Other consequences that flow from the prescript being considered here are, as stated by Father Larraona:

---

[8] Cf. above, p. 152.

[9] Generally, higher superiors are not allowed to obligate the property of inferior moral persons without informing the immediate superior of this moral person. However, the consent of this superior is not always necessary.

a) There is no necessity for the superior whose permission is required for a transaction to state in granting it that he is or is not accepting responsibility for it.

b) The other party to the contract need not be informed that responsibility is limited to the party contracting; nor need he be shown documents showing that the consent of superiors has been obtained for the transaction.[10]

7. In all that has been said "good faith" is presupposed. Any action by which the invalidity of a contract would be induced in order to avoid responsibility would, of course, fail of its effect. Likewise, the transfer of property to another moral person, in order that the contracting person should thereby become incapable of fulfilling its obligations, would only transfer the obligation to the recipient of the property.

2. RESPONSIBILITY OF RELIGIOUS ACTING WITH PERMISSION.

I. *Regulars*

> § 2. "*Si contraxerit regularis cum licentia Superiorum, respondere debet persona moralis, cuius Superior licentiam dedit;* . . ."—Canon 536.

Having considered in paragraph 1 the responsibility for debts and obligations contracted in the name of a religious moral person, the Code in paragraph 2 of this canon considers the responsibility for obligations incurred by a religious in his own name and not as an agent of his community or institute. The first part of this paragraph deals with regulars.

1. As a preliminary to this prescript it should be stated that a religious before taking solemn vows must within sixty days of his solemn profession, but conditioned upon it, give up the own-

[10] "Commentarium Codicis," *CpR*, XIV (1933), 424. It will be prudent at times for superiors to make an express declaration denying responsibility.

ership of any property he may have, and while in solemn vows he lacks capacity to acquire any property.[11]

From this it is seen that a regular cannot on his own authority validly take upon himself as a regular an economic obligation, for the reason that he lacks the actual means and the future hope of satisfying that obligation.[12] In order to contract a valid obligation the regular must have the permission of his legitimate superior. The Code then states that when a regular has this permission the responsibility for the obligation contracted by the regular rests with the moral person *whose superior gave the permission.*

2. It should be noted in regard to this:

a) That the responsibility does not necessarily attach to the moral person or community to which the regular belongs, but to the moral person from whose superior the regular obtained the permission; e. g., if the provincial gave the permission, the province is responsible, not the house to which the regular belongs;[13]

---

[11] Cf. canons 581; 582. The Holy See can of course dispense from this law.

[12] When the law imposes a condition that removes capacity to satisfy an obligation, it must logically be understood as removing capacity to contract an obligation, otherwise the law would be conniving at an evident injustice. It may be debated whether or not the Code considers the religious of simple vows as one having capacity to contract obligations notwithstanding his vows (cf. below, p. 170). But there should be no doubt that this is lacking to the regular with solemn vows:

"Ma ben diversamente va la cosa per un religioso, specialmente di voti solenni. Questi, come si e detto di sopra, non ha nè il *velle,* nè il *nolle.* Quindi non ha personalità giuridica propria, nè i superiori possono conferirgliela perchè contraria ai voti."—S.C. de Rel., 18 Aug. 1914—*AAS,* VII (1915), 110. Hence, authors who speak of the contracts of regulars as *illicit* if made without permission must be understood as referring to the contracts of the individuals. As contracts of regulars they are invalid.

[13] Note, however, that if the provincial superior merely authorizes a local superior to allow one of his subjects to contract an obligation, it is really the local superior who is giving the permission and therefore the house,

b) That the responsibility does not attach to the moral person unless the superior giving the permission fulfills all that is required for the validity of an act by which the moral person he represents is to be obligated; and unless the regular fulfills those things prescribed for the validity of his transaction;

c) That the permission may be express or tacit. Thus, if the acts of the regular are public and notorious, as for instance obligations resulting from the publication of a periodical, the permission of superiors is at least tacit, if they have not publicly and expressly refused to take responsibility. At the same time they cannot permit the regular to contract the obligations unless they are willing to accept the responsibility. Any agreement contrary to this existing between the regular and his superior is without value.[14]

3. If the act is merely illicit, either on the part of the superior giving the permission, or on the part of the regular performing it, the moral person from whose superior the permission was obtained is responsible. But the competent superior can punish the delinquent.[15]

4. A question may be raised about the extent of this prescript. The Code says "*si contraxerit regularis.*" The technical meaning of '*regularis*' is "one who has pronounced vows in an order."[16] In this sense it makes no difference whether the vows pronounced have been simple or solemn. By way of contrast the Code designates those who pronounce vows in a congregation as "*religiosi votorum simplicium.*"[17] Now since the Code uses both terms in evident contrast in canon 536 § 2, it is logical to take them at their legal value and to consider the term 'regular'

---

not the province, is responsible. Cf. Larraona, *op. cit.*, XV (1934), 21; Wernz-Vidal, *Jus Can.*, III, 182.

[14] Cf. S.C. de Rel., *Diocesis seu Ordinis N.*, 18 Aug. 1914—*AAS*, VII (1915), 104-112.

[15] Cf. Berutti, *Institutiones J.C.*, III, 126.

[16] Canon 488,7°.

[17] *Ibid.*

as applicable to all religious who pronounce vows in an order, whether their vows are simple or solemn.[18] However, many authors oppose this view on the grounds that the professed with simple vows in an order have capacity to own and acquire property and therefore there is no sound reason for making the order responsible for their obligations.[19]

Certainly the opinion of the eminent authors who hold this view merits the highest consideration. But, is it not possible that the merits of the question should be decided not on the capacity to own, but on the capacity to use and dispose of property? All professed with simple vows have capacity to own and acquire property.[20] To a limited extent they have capacity to use and dispose of this property.[21] But does this capacity to use and dispose flow from the ownership or is it a concession granted by the eccelsiastical authorities? If the latter, could not the legislator make the concession to those professed in a congregation without extending it to those professed (even with simple vows) in an order?

The source of this prescript, as noted in Cardinal Gasparri's edition of the Code, makes it quite evident that religious with solemn vows have no juridical capacity. The matter is not so clear in regard to regulars with simple vows.[22]

II. *Religious With Simple Vows*

> "*Si* [*contraxerit*] *religiosus votorum simplicium, ipse respondere debet, nisi de Superioris licentia negotium religionis gesserit.*"—Canon 536 § 2.

---

[18] Cf. Blat, *De Personis*, p. 584; Oesterle, *Praelectiones*, p. 281.

[19] Cf. Vermeersch-Creusen, *Epitome*, I, n. 661; Mayer, *Benediktinisches Ordensrecht*, II, 299; Schaefer, *De Religiosis*, p. 346; Larraona, *op. cit.*, p. 18.

[20] Canon 580 § 1.

[21] Canon 580 § 3; 583—Note that can. 583 refers to professed with simple vows in a congregation.

[22] Cf. above, p. 169, note 12.

The second part of paragraph 2 considers the obligations contracted by religious with simple vows. If the terminology of the Code is taken in its legal meaning, then by religious of simple vows are meant only those professed in a religious congregation. However, as already stated, the exact extent of this prescript is doubtful and there are many prominent canonists favoring the opinion that it extends to all professed with simple vows whether they belong to an order or a congregation.[23]

The Code states:

1. That religious of simple vows are themselves responsible for obligations which they contract in their own name and not as agents of their religious house, province, or institute. This is true even though they incur the obligations with the consent of their legitimate superior.

2. Because of the individual's responsibility, the house, province, or institute cannot be held responsible for these obligations, even though the individual lack the means with which to satisfy them. The method of collecting is the concern of the creditor who, as in all such cases, accepts the risk in making the contract. The permission of the superior is in this case to be understood only as the removal of any obstacle to the licitness of the contract, which is valid even without the permission.[24]

If the religious of simple vows is engaged in the affairs of his institute, the moral person whose superior gave the mandate is responsible for obligations incurred by the religious. In this case, however, the permission has to be validly given and the action of the religious must be within the limits of his mandate. As already stated, a superior cannot, without at the same time accepting the responsibility, give permission to a subject to contract an obligation in matters that pertain to the institute. Likewise, he tacitly accepts responsibility when he becomes aware that a religious is contracting obligations in affairs that

[23] Cf. above, p. 171, note 19.

[24] Canon 579.

pertain to the institute, and he issues no prohibitions in regard to them.[25]

3. RESPONSIBILITY OF RELIGIOUS ACTING WITHOUT PERMISSION.

> § 3. "*Si contraxerit religiosus sine ulla Superiorum licentia, ipsemet respondere debet, non autem religio vel provincia vel domus.*"—Canon 536.

The third paragraph of canon 536 refers to obligations contracted by religious without the required permission. As is clear, the prescript extends to all religious whether of solemn or simple vows, whether they act in their own name or pretend to act in the name of their institute; and to superiors as well as subjects, because the act of a superior, who in acting exceeds his competence, is as little capable of obligating the moral person he represents as is the act of a subject. The norms to be used in determining whether or not the moral person is obligated are common and particular law.[26]

The Code uses the words *sine ulla Superiorum licentia* and some authors have interpreted this to mean that any presumed or implicit or tacit permission is sufficient to obligate the moral person.[27] Yet, as Larraona points out, the logic of the canon is opposed to this. Paragraph 3 is complementary to §§ 1, 2, and should not be interpreted as allowing the choice of any kind of permission.[28] Canon 534 is precise in stating the permission required for contracting obligations, and the solemnities, as stated there, should not be omitted for light reasons. However,

---

[25] Cf. p. 170.

[26] Bastien, *Directoire Canonique*, n. 371; Larraona, o. c., p. 110.

[27] Cf. Oesterle, *Praelectiones J.C.*, p. 281; Fanfani, *De Jure Relig.*, n. 166; Wernz-Vidal, *Jus Canonicum*, III, n. 232; Schaefer, *De Religiosis*, p. 346; Schoensteiner, *Grundriss des Ordensrechts*, p. 241.

[28] *Op. cit.*, p. 111.

as stated elsewhere,[29] and apparently confirmed in the resolution of the case proposed to a special Commission of Cardinals,[30] it is not certain that all solemnities of canon 534 are necessary for the validity of a contract obligating a moral person, because, as stated by the Commission. *"se i superiore lo lasciano fare deve dirse che l'autorizanno"*;[31] i. e., even though they have not given express and written permission. On the other hand, the superior must in some way be aware that the obligation is being contracted in the name of the moral person before it can be said that he has given consent.

If the superior has not given his consent to an obligation contracted by his subject, the moral person represented by the superior cannot be held responsible for the obligation. The responsibility rests on the religious himself whether he has solemn or simple vows. The way in which the obligation is to be satisfied must be determined by the creditor.

By obligation is meant not only that which arises from a contract or quasi-contract, but also that which arises from a delict or from an accident or injury to the property or person of another, and resulting from actions performed without the permission of the superior.[32]

4. ACTION FOR RECOVERY OF DAMAGES.

> § 4. *"Firmum tamen semper esto, contra eum, in cuius rem aliquid ex inito contractu versum est, semper posse actionem institui."*—Can. 536.

After having stated the rules which govern the responsibility as well of the moral person as of the individual religious, canon

[29] Above, pp. 127-131.

[30] S.C. de Rel., *Dioecesis seu Ordinis N.*, 18 Aug. 1914—*AAS*, VII (1915), 104-112.

[31] *Ibid.* p. 108.

[32] "Delictum personae non debet in detrimentum ecclesiae redundare."—Reg. 76, *R.J.*, *in VI°*.

536 in paragraph 4 considers the possibility of injury or damages resulting from the contract and states that the one injured may take action against the person profiting from the contract, whether the person be a party to the contract or not.

By way of example, let it be supposed that A sells to B, the superior of a religious house, an article worth five hundred dollars. The article is acquired by the house of which B is superior. But B cannot validly obligate his community to the extent of five hundred dollars without the permission of his provincial, which in the case has not been obtained. B therefore is personally responsible to A for the five hundred dollars. If A cannot collect from B, A is allowed to take action against the community for the recovery of the article or the value of it. If A can collect from B, then B is entitled to take action against the community for the recovery of the article or its value, because even though not responsible for an obligation invalidly contracted, the community is in no case allowed to profit from that contract at the expense of another. Similar examples may be imagined where the community would be allowed to take action against another for loss or damages sustained.[33]

This action which is an extended application of the Roman Law *actio de in rem verso,* can be taken in the ecclesiastical court, or also in the civil court if the proper permissions have been obtained.[34] It should be noted however that the Holy See will sometimes oblige the moral person to satisfy the obligations of a contract if its invalidity is due to the neglect or incompetence of the religious administrator and the other party to the contract has been in good faith. This is necessary to preserve

[33] Cf. Berutti, *Institutiones J.C.*, III, 128.

[34] Cf. canon 120. In Roman Law the *actio de in rem verso* was allowed only to the creditor against the *paterfamilias* or *dominus* for damages resulting from contracts with a son or a slave. Cf. C. (4, 26); D. (15, 13); Larraona, *op. cit.*, XV (1934), 204, note. 842.

the good name of the Church and of ecclesiastical moral persons.[85]

5. DUTY OF SUPERIORS IN REGARD TO DEBTS AND OBLIGATIONS.

> § 5. "*Caveant Superiores religiosi ne debita contrahenda permittant, nisi certo constet ex consuetis reditibus posse debiti foenus solvi et intra tempus non nimis longum per legitimam amortizationem reddi summam capitalem.*"—Canon 536.

The final paragraph of canon 536 is a reminder to religious superiors of their individual responsibilities as administrators and representatives of the moral person entrusted to their care, to see to it that the moral person suffers no injury or loss of prestige or of the good opinion of others through mismanaged affairs, especially in the economic order. As a safeguard, religious superiors may not permit that any debts be contracted in the name of the moral person they represent or over which they have jurisdiction, unless it be *reasonably certain* that the *regular* income of the moral person will be sufficient, not only to pay the annual interest on the debt but also to repay the principal within a period of time that is not too extended.

By the regular income is to be understood salary, stole fees, income from property, customary donations, etc. The *hope* of a donation or of a gift from some generous benefactor gives no reasonable certainty, and therefore *is not justification for contracting a debt!*[86]

---

[85] Cf. above, p. 131.

[86] "Quae . . . regulis christianae prudentiae et aequae administrationis non semper respondeant, ideoque apostolicarum praescriptionum verbis et spiritui contraria sint, Deo esse grata non possunt, nec proximo valent permansuram afferre utilitatem."—S.C. de Rel., instr. *Inter ea*, July 30, 1909, § 1—*AAS*, I (1909), 695.

The amortization of a debt means the setting aside at regular intervals of a certain amount of money or its equivalent for the purpose of providing for the liquidation of the debt at or before maturity. The money thus set aside may be profitably deposited or invested as an aid towards the payment of the debt. Another amortization plan is to pay the interest due and part of the principal in regular installments, so that in time the debt will be entirely extinguished.[37] When permission for debts must be obtained from the Holy See, the plan of amortization must be sent with the petition.[38]

The Code states that the debt should be extinguished in a period of time that is not too extended. Twenty to thirty years may be considered as not too long a time,[39] and special circumstances, as the danger of confiscation, may justify a longer period.[40]

---

[37] Cf. Hoagland, *Corporation Finance,* McGraw-Hill: New York, 1933, p. 102.

[38] Letter of the Apostolic Deelgate to Religious Superiors, § IV, n. 4.

[39] Berutti, *Institutiones J.C.,* III, 128.

[40] Larraona, *op. cit.,* XV (1934), 206.

CHAPTER VII

DONATIONS

CANON 537

"*Largitiones ex bonis domus, provinciae, religionis non permittuntur, nisi ratione eleemosynae vel alia iusta de causa, de venia Superioris et ad normam constitutionum.*"—Canon 537.

The practical application of canon 537 is left to the determination of the constitutions of the various religious institutes, and lacking these, to the religious superiors. Pope Clement VIII in 1594 prohibited regulars of either sex under severe penalties from making donations of the goods of the monastery without the consent of the General Chapter.[1] But as this law was too rigorous, Pope Urban VIII in 1640 declared that religious could make donations in the name of the monastery for reasons of gratitude, or to gain or retain the good will of others towards their convent or institute, or for other causes having virtue or merit. But the donations were to be moderate and not too frequent and never to be given without the permission of the local superior and other permissions required by the constitutions.[2] The regulations of Urban VIII were in substance renewed by the Sacred Congregation of Religious in 1909[3] and have also found their way into the Code in canon 537. According to this canon, donations made from the goods of the house, province, or institute are permitted: (1) as an alms, e. g., to the poor, to hospitals, to churches for divine worship, etc.; (2)

---

[1] Const. *"Religiosae Congregationes,"* 19 June 1594—*Fontes*, n. 178.

[2] Const. *"Nuper,"* 16 Oct. 1640, § 1—*Fontes*, n. 220.

[3] Instr. *Inter ea*, July 30, 1909, § XIII—*Fontes*, n. 4394.

for other just causes, e. g., a gratuity for services rendered; a donation for civic and patriotic celebrations in order to obtain or retain the good will of the community; a donation in time of floods, earthquakes, fires, etc., as an aid to the sufferers. Donations of this sort, even if made with money belonging to the community, are licit, provided the permission of the superior has been obtained and the norms set down in the constitutions have been observed. Under other circumstances a donation of the property of the community places the donor under the obligation to make restitution to the community. If a religious of solemn vows, he must make an effort to have the recipient return the donation or its value. However, good faith, poverty, the smallness of the donation, and other circumstances on the part of the recipient will often excuse from this obligation. If a religious of simple vows makes a donation without permission, he must make restitution to the community out of his own means, unless the recipient restores the donation or its value.[4]

The penalties formerly inflicted on those who donated to others the property of the monastery are not mentioned in the Code and are therefore abrogated.[5] However, penalties prescribed by the various constitutions retain their force and may be applied.[6]

As a conclusion to this chapter the following practical suggestions are quoted from the *Commentary* of Augustine:

> It may be added that tips to waiters or porters, small gifts as gratuities, etc., do not oblige to restitution, and if made for a good reason, are not against poverty. Religious articles, such as medals, pictures, etc., may be given without fear of violating poverty. A religious when travelling is allowed to act like a gentleman towards those whose help or assistance or good will he needs. Finally, canon 537 allows donations to be

[4] Augustine, *A Commentary,* III, 196.

[5] Canon 6,5°.

[6] Berutti, *Institutiones J.C.,* III, 129.

made as alms or for any just reason, provided the superior consents. This consent may be presumed in cases of urgency or necessity. Too rigid an insistance upon poverty when charity calls is against the very groundwork of religion. Religious are not to be stingy, but the saying of the Apostle was also intended for them: "It is a more blessed thing to give than to receive" (Acts XX, 35). Besides, every religious community has a social position to fill and a social duty to live up to. The ancient monasteries were fully aware of this great and noble task.[7]

---

[7] Augustine, *A Commentary,* III, 196-197.

CONCLUSION

The history of the temporal goods of religious institutes, as traced in these pages, has not been dedicated to proving the need for temporal goods. This has been assumed throughout, since the religious institute is but kin to most institutes and organizations in needing the use and possession of temporal goods for the attainment of its proper end. But starting from the fact of possession, the purpose has been to show that the Church law as found in conciliar and papal enactments has sanctioned and defended the natural right of religious institutes not only to use and possess, but even to own temporal goods. That some institutes, following an ideal, have renounced absolutely the ownership of property, in no wise touches the right of other institutes. That some political entities have tried to deny to religious institutes their right to legitimately acquired possessions is due in most instances to ill-will or avarice, and has no valid arguments to recommend or explain it. The present Code of Canon Law reiterates the former law of the Church in regard to the right of religious institutes to acquire and possess property, stressing, perhaps more than was formerly done, the legal right of ecclesiastical moral persons in regard to temporal possessions. In the commentary special attention has been given to the particular moral persons that go to make up a religious institute.

As to what concerns the administration of temporal goods, history shows that first the founders of the institutes by their rules and constitutions, and later the Church itself by wise and prudent laws, have sought to regulate, according to persons and circumstances, the action of administrators; but in a way that would allow the maximum of liberty to the religious organization while safeguarding the interests not only of the institute, but also of the Church of which it forms a part. As the religious state developed and new problems arose the Church has tried to meet the changed conditions with new laws suited to the circumstances. What these laws have been, and when they arose, this study has tried to point out in the historical outline. In the commentary a general outline has first been given of the various subjects of administration with their respective rights and duties; then, passing to particular phases of administration, attention was paid to investments, alienations, debts and obligations, the account of administration and the responsibility for administrative acts.

Not all phases of these subjects have been considered. The principal object of canons 533-535 is to define the authority of external ecclesiastical superiors over acts performed by the administrators of religious institutes. In regard to investments it was seen that over these the Code gives to the local ordinary a certain amount of vigilance. However, the law is of general application only in regard to nuns and diocesan sisterhoods. Other religious are subject to the law of canon 533 only in particular cases such as the investment of the dowry, of donations for local charities, of parish funds.

The law governing alienation and the contracting of debts and obligations is of a more general character, since its main features are applicable to all religious without exception. The distinctions made in the canon have in view the nature of the act rather than the quality of the religious performing it. The formalities which are prescribed for acts that tend to lessen the economic independence of religious moral persons, clearly show the concern of the Church to safeguard the economic stability of religious institutes in order that the spiritual good which these institutes may accomplish be not impeded by temporal considerations.

The account of administration is an additional aid and safeguard to efficient and prudent administration. But as it is stated in canon 535, it is of obligation only in those cases wherein the local ordinary may exercise his jurisdiction either by reason of the persons or the property concerned. In other cases religious must account directly to the Holy See; for none are entirely exempt from supervision in administrative matters.

Canon 536 fixes the responsibility for obligations contracted by religious whether they act in their own name or in the name of the religious moral person. In regard to this matter the Code is precise and clarifies a law which formerly was not too clear. As an appendix to this canon the Code gives a warning to religious superiors to be circumspect in the matter of contracting debts and to give special attention to the manner in which they are to be repaid. Title X concludes by indicating that reasonable donations are permitted in accordance with the norms laid down in the constitutions of the various religious institutes.

ALPHABETICAL INDEX

BIOGRAPHICAL NOTE

JAMES E. MCMANUS was born in Brooklyn, New York, October 10, 1900 and attended there the Parochial School of Our Lady of Perpetual Help. In 1921 he graduated from St. Mary's College, North East, Pennsylvania; entered the Novitiate of the Redemptorist Fathers at Ilchester, Maryland, and the following year made his religious profession as a member of the Congregation of the Most Holy Redeemer. After his course of studies, made at the Redemptorist Seminary, Esopus, New York, he was ordained to the priesthood, June 19, 1927. In September, 1934, he entered the Catholic University of America to pursue a graduate course of studies in the School of Canon Law. He received the degree of Baccalaureate in Canon Law in 1935, and the degree of Licentiate in Canon Law in 1936.

CANON LAW STUDIES

1. Frebiks, Rev. Celestine A., C.PP.S., J.C.D., Religious Congregations in Their External Relations, 121 pp., 1916.
2. Galliher, Rev. Daniel M., O.P., J.C.D., Canonical Elections, 117 pp., 1917.
3. Borkowski, Rev. Aurelius L., O.F.M., De Confraternitatibus Ecclesiasticis, 136 pp., 1918.
4. Castillo, Rev. Cayo, J.C.D., Disertacion Historico-canonica sobre la Potestad del Cabildo en Sede Vacante o Impedida del Vicario Capitular 99 pp., 1919 (1918).
5. Kubelbeck, Rev. William J., S.T.B., J.C.D., The Sacred Penitentiaria and Its Relations to Faculties of Ordinaries and Priests, 129 pp., 1918.
6. Petrovits, Rev. Joseph J. C., S.T.D., J.C.D., The New Church Law on Matrimony, X-461 pp., 1919.
7. Hickey, Rev. John J., S.T.B., J.C.D., Irregularities and Simple Impediments in the New Code of Canon Law, 100 pp., 1920.
8. Klekotka, Rev. Peter J., S.T.B., J.C.D., Diocesan Consultors, 179 pp., 1920.
9. Wannenmacher, Rev. Francis, J.C.D., The Evidence in Ecclesiastical Procedure Affecting the Marriage Bond, 1920. (Printed 1935.)
10. Golden, Rev. Henry Francis, J.C.D., Parochial Benefices in the New Code, IV-119 pp., 1921. (Printed 1925.)
11. Koudelka, Rev. Charles J., J.C.D., Pastors, Their Rights and Duties According to the New Code of Canon Law, 211 pp., 1921.
12. Melo, Rev. Antonius, O.F.M., J.C.D., De Exemptione Regularium, X-188 pp., 1921.
13. Schaff, Rev. Valentine Theodore, O.F.M., S.T.B., J.C.D., The Cloister, X-180 pp., 1921.
14. Burke, Rev. Thomas Joseph, S.T.B., J.C.D., Competence in Ecclesiastical Tribunals, IV-117 pp., 1922.
15. Leech, Rev. George Leo, J.C.D., A Comparative Study of the Constitution, "Apostolicae Sedis" and the "Codex Juris Canonici," 179 pp., 1922.
16. Motry, Rev. Hubert Louis, S.T.D., J.C.D., Diocesan Faculties According to the Code of Canon Law, II-167 pp., 1922.
17. Murphy, Rev. George Lawrence, J.C.D., Delinquencies and Penalties in the Administration and the Reception of the Sacraments, IV-121 pp., 1923.

18. O'Reilly, Rev. John Anthony, S.T.B., J.C.D., Ecclesiastical Sepulture in the New Code of Canon Law, II-129 pp., 1923.

19. Michalicka, Rev. Wenceslas Cyrill, O.S.B., J.C.D., Judicial Procedure in Dismissal of Clerical Exempt Religious, 107 pp., 1923.

20. Dargin, Rev. Edward Vincent, S.T.B., J.C.D., Reserved Cases According to the Code of Canon Law, IV-103 pp., 1924.

21. Godfrey, Rev. John A., S.T.B., J.C.D., The Right of Patronage According to the Code of Canon Law, 153 pp., 1924.

22. Hagedorn, Rev. Francis Edward, J.C.D., General Legislation on Indulgences, II-154 pp., 1924.

23. King, Rev. James Ignatius, J.C.D., The Administration of the Sacraments to Dying Non-Catholics, V-141 pp., 1924.

24. Winslow, Rev. Francis Joseph, O.F.M., J.C.D., Vicars and Prefects Apostolic, IV-149 pp., 1924.

25. Correa, Rev. Jose Servelion, S.T.L., J.C.D., La Potestad Legislativa de la Iglesia Catolica, IV-127 pp., 1925.

26. Dugan, Rev. Henry Francis, M.A., J.C.D., The Judiciary Department of the Diocesan Curia, 87 pp., 1925.

27. Keller, Rev. Charles Frederick, S.T.B., J.C.D., Mass Stipends, 167 pp., 1925.

28. Paschang, Rev. John Linus, J.C.D., The Sacramentals According to the Code of Canon Law, 129 pp., 1925.

29. Pointek, Rev. Cyrillus, O.F.M., S.T.B., J.C.D., De Indulto Exclaustrationis necnon Saecularizationis, XIII-289 pp., 1925.

30. Kearney, Rev. Richard Joseph, S.T.D., J.C.D., Sponsors at Baptism According to the Code of Canon Law, IV-127 pp., 1925.

31. Bartlett, Rev. Chester Joseph, A.M., LL.B., J.C.D., The Tenure of Parochial Property in the United States of America, V-108 pp., 1926.

32. Kilker, Rev. Adrian Jerome, J.C.D., Extreme Unction, V-425 pp., 1926.

33. McCormick, Rev. Robert Emmett, J.C.D., Confessors of Religious, VIII-266 pp., 1926.

34. Miller, Rev. Newton Thomas, J.C.D., Founded Masses According to the Code of Canon Law, VIII-93 pp., 1926.

35. Roelker, Rev. Edward G., S.T.D., J.C.D., Principles of Privilege According to the Code of Canon Law, XI-166 pp., 1926.

36. Bakalarczyk, Rev. Richardus, M.I.C., J.U.D., De Novitiatu, VIII-208 pp., 1927.

37. Pizzuti, Rev. Lawrence, O.F.M., J.U.L., De Parochis Religiosis, 1927. (Not Printed.)

38. Bliley, Rev. Nicholas Martin, O.S.B., J.C.D., Altars According to the Code of Canon Law, XIX-132 pp., 1927.
39. Brown, Brendan Francis, A.L., LL.M., J.U.D., The Canonical Juristic Personality with Special Reference to its Status in the United States of America, V-212 pp., 1927.
40. Cavanaugh, Rev. William Thomas, C.P., J.U.D., The Reservation of the Blessed Sacrament, VIII-101 pp., 1927.
41. Doheny, Rev. William J., C.S.C., A.B., J.U.D., Church Property: Modes of Acquisition, X-118 pp., 1927.
42. Feldhaus, Rev. Aloysius H., C.PP.C., J.C.D., Oratories, IX-141 pp., 1927.
43. Kelly, Rev. James Patrick, A.B., J.C.D., The Jurisdiction of the Simple Confessor, X-208 pp., 1927.
44. Neuberger, Rev. Nicholas J., J.C.D., Canon 6 or the Relation of the Codex Juris Canonici to the Preceding Legislation, V-95 pp., 1927.
45. O'Keefe, Rev. Gerald Michael, J.C.D., Matrimonial Dispensations, Powers of Bishops, Priests, and Confessors, VIII-232 pp., 1927.
46. Quigley, Rev. Joseph, A.M., A.B., J.C.D., Condemned Societies, 139 pp., 1927.
47. Zaplotnik, Rev. Ioannes Leo, J.C.D., De Vicariis Foraneis, X-142 pp., 1927.
48. Duskie, Rev. John Aloysius, A.B., J.C.D., The Canonical Status of the Orientals in the United States, VIII-196 pp., 1928.
49. Hyland, Rev. Francis Edward, J.C.D., Excommunication, Its Nature, Historical Development and Effects, VIII-181 pp., 1928.
50. Reinmann, Rev. Gerald Joseph, O.M.C., J.C.D., The Third Order Secular of Saint Francis, 201 pp., 1928.
51. Schenk, Rev. Francis J., J.C.D., The Matrimonial Impediments of Mixed Religion and Disparity of Cult, XVI-318 pp., 1929.
52. Coady, Rev. John Joseph, S.T.D., J.U.D., A.M., The Appointment of Pastors, VIII-150 pp., 1929.
53. Kay, Rev. Thomas Henry, J.C.D., Competence in Matrimonial Procedure, VIII-164 pp., 1929.
54. Turner, Rev. Sidney Joseph, C.P., J.U.D., The Vow of Poverty, XLIX-217 pp., 1929.
55. Kearney, Rev. Raymond A., A.B., S.T.D., J.C.D., The Principles of Delegation, VII-149 pp., 1929.
56. Conran, Rev Edward James, A.B., J.C.D., The Interdict, V-163 pp., 1930.
57. O'Neil, Rev. William H., J.C.D., Papal Rescripts of Favor, VII-218 pp., 1930.

58. Bastnagel, Rev. Clement Vincent, J.U.D., The Appointment of Parochial Adjutants and Assistants, XV-257 pp., 1930.

59. Ferry, Rev. William A., A.B., J.C.D., Stole Fees, X-107 pp., 1930.

60. Costello, Rev. John Michael, A.M., J.C.D., Domicile and Quasi-Domicile, VII-201 pp., 1930.

61. Kremer, Rev. Michael Nicholas, A.B., S.T.B., J.C.D., Church Support in the United States, VI-136 pp., 1930.

62. Angulo, Rev, Luis, C.M., J.C.D., Legislacion de la Iglesia sobre la intenciôn en la applicaciôn de la Santa Misa, VII-104 pp., 1931.

63. Frey, Rev. Wolfgang Norbert, O.S.B., A.B., J.C.D., The Act of Religious Profession, VIII-174 pp., 1931.

64. Roberts, Rev. James Brendan, A.B., J.C.D., The Bans of Marriage, XIV-140 pp., 1931.

65. Ryder, Rev. Raymond Aloysius, A.B., J.C.D., Simony, IX-151 pp., 1931.

66. Campagna, Rev. Angelo, Ph.D., J.U.D., Il Vicario Generale del Vescovo, VII-205 pp., 1931.

67. Cox, Rev. Joseph Godfrey, A.B., J.C.D., The Administration of Seminaries, VI-124 pp., 1931.

68. Gregory, Rev. Donald J., J.U.D., The Pauline Privilege, XV-165 pp., 1931.

69. Donohue, Rev. John F., J.C.D., The Impediment of Crime, VIII-110 pp., 1931.

70. Dooley, Rev. Eugene A., O.M.I., J.C.D., Church Law on Sacred Relics, IX-143 pp., 1931.

71. Orth, Rev. Clement Raymond, O.C.M., J.C.D., The Approbation of Religious Institutes, 171 pp., 1931.

72. Pernicone, Rev. Joseph M., A.B., J.C.D., The Ecclesiastical Prohibition of Books, XII-267 pp., 1932.

73. Clinton, Rev. Connell, A.B., J.C.D., The Pascal Precept, IX-108 pp., 1932.

74. Donnelly, Rev. Francis B., A.M., S.T.L., J.C.D., The Diocesan Synod, VIII-125 pp., 1932.

75. Torrente, Rev. Camilo, C.F.M., J.C.D., Las Processiones Sagradas, V-145 pp., 1932.

76. Murphy, Rev. Edwin J., C.PP.S., J.C.D., Suspension Ex Informata Conscientia, XI-122 pp., 1932.

77. MacKenzie, Rev. Eric F., A.M., S.T.L., J.C.D., The Delict of Heresy in its Commission, Penalization, Absolution, VII-124 pp., 1932.

78. Lyons, Rev. Avitus E., S.T.B., J.C.D., The Collegiate Tribunal of First Instance, XI-147 pp., 1932.

79. Connolly, Rev. Thomas A., J.C.D., Appeals, XI-195 pp., 1932.

80. SANGMEISTER, REV. JOSEPH V., A.B., J.C.D., Force and Fear as Precluding Matrimonial Consent, V-211 pp., 1932.
81. JAEGER, REV. LEO A., A.B., J.C.D., The Administration of Vacant and Quasi-Vacant Episcopal Sees in the United States, IX-229 pp., 1932.
82. RIMLINGER, REV. HERBERT T., J.C.D., Error Invalidating Matrimonial Consent, VII-79 pp., 1932.
83. BARRETT, REV. JOHN D. M., S.S., J.C.D., Comparative Study of the Third Plenary Council and the Code, IX-221 pp., 1932.
84. CARBERRY, REV. JOHN J., PHD., S.T.D., J.C.D., The Juridical Form of Marriage, X-177 pp., 1934.
85. DOLAN, REV. JOHN L., A.B., J.C.D., The Defensor Vinculi, XII-157 pp., 1934.
86. HANNAN, REV. JEROME D., A.M., S.T.D., LL.B., J.C.D., The Canon Law of Wills, IX-517 pp., 1934.
87. LEMIEUX, REV. DELISLE A., A.M., J.C.D., The Sentence in Ecclesiastical Procedure, IX-131 pp., 1934.
88. O'ROURKE, REV. JAMES J., A.B., J.C.D., Parish Registers, VII-109 pp., 1934.
89. TIMLIN, REV. BARTHOLOMEW, O.F.M., A.M., J.C.D., Conditional Matrimonial Consent, X-381 pp., 1924.
90. WAHL, REV. FRANCIS X., A.B., J.C.D., The Matrimonial Impediments of Consanguinity and Affinity, VI-125 pp., 1935.
91. WHITE, REV. ROBERT J., A.B., LL.B., S.T.B., J.C.D., Canonical Ante-Nuptial Promises and the Civil Law, V-152 pp., 1934.
92. HERRERA, REV. ANTONIO PARRA, O.C.D., J.C.D., Legislacion Ecclesiastica sobre el Ayuno y la Abstinencia, XI-191 pp., 1935.
93. KENNEDY, REV. EDWIN J., J.C.D., The Special Matrimonial Process in Cases of Evident Nullity, X-165 pp., 1935.
94. MANNING, REV. JOHN J., A.B., J.C.D., Presumption of Law in Matrimonial Procedure, XI-111 pp., 1935.
95. MOEDER, REV. JOHN M., J.C.D., The Proper Bishop for Ordination and Dimissorial Letters, VII-135 pp., 1935.
96. O'MARA, REV. WILLIAM A., A.B., J.C.D., Canonical Causes for Matrimonial Dispensations, IX-155 pp., 1935.
97. REILLY, REV. PETER, J.C.D., Residence of Pastors, IX-81 pp., 1935.
98. SMITH, REV. MARINER T., O.P., S.T.LR., J.C.D., The Penal Law for Religious, VII-169 pp., 1935.
99. WHALEN, REV. DONALD W., A.M., J.C.D., The Value of Testimonial Evidence in Matrimonial Procedure, XIII-297 pp., 1935.
100. CLEARY, REV. JOSEPH F., J.C.D., Canonical Limitations on the Alienation of Church Property, VIII-141 pp., 1936.

101. GLYNN, REV. JOHN C., J.C.D., The Promoter of Justice, XX-337 pp., 1936.
102. BRENNAN, REV. JAMES, S.S., J.C.L., The Simple Convalidation of Marriage, 1937.
103. BRUNINI, REV. JOSEPH BERNARD, A.B., S.T.B., J.C.L., Clerical Obligations of Canons 139 and 142, 1937.
104. CONNOR, REV. MAURICE, J.C.L., The Administrative Removal of Pastors, 1937.
105. GUILFOYLE, REV. MERLIN JOSEPH, J.C.L., Custom, 1937.
106. HUGHES, REV. JAMES A., A.B., A.M., J.C.L., Witnesses in Criminal Trials of Clerics, 1937.
107. JANSEN, REV. RAYMOND J., A.B., S.T.L., J.C.L., Canonical Provisions for Cathetical Instruction, 1937.
108. KEALY, REV. JOHN J., A.B,, J. C. L., The Introductory Libellus, 1937.
109. MCMANUS, REV. JAMES EDWARD, C.SS.R., J.C.L., The Administration of Temporal Goods in Religious Institutes, 1937.
110. MORIARTY, REV. EUGENE JAMES, J.C.L., Oaths in Ecclesiastical Courts, 1937.
111. RAINER, REV. ELIGIUS GEORGE, C.SS.R., J.C.L., Suspension of Clerics, 1937.
112. REILLY, REV. THOMAS F., C.SS.R, J.C.L., Visitation of Religious, 1937.

www.ingramcontent.com/pod-product-compliance
Lightning Source LLC
LaVergne TN
LVHW050239080826
844660LV00012B/563